Jesus by Numbers

Lloyd Daggett

WestBow·
PRESS
A DIVISION OF THOMAS NELSON
& ZONDERVAN

WestBow Press books may be ordered through booksellers or by contacting:

WestBow Press
A Division of Thomas Nelson & Zondervan
1663 Liberty Drive
Bloomington, IN 47403
www.westbowpress.com
1 (866) 928-1240

ISBN: 978-1-4908-2376-8 (sc)
ISBN: 978-1-4908-2375-1 (e)

Library of Congress Control Number: 2014901409

Printed in the United States of America.

WestBow Press rev. date: 12/08/2014

Contents

About the Author

I grew up as a preacher's kid in a little town in Oregon. I have had many opportunities to witness how God works. The times I saw the hand of God in my life were always surprising, and yet they weren't. I was a prodigal son several times in my life, times when I chose my own path, but I will have eternal gratitude for the fact that God never left me and was quick to welcome me back with outstretched arms.

In my late twenties, I met Delbert Powers, a man who challenged and changed my walk with God. One subject he was interested in was the usage of repeated numbers in the Word of God such as the numbers three, seven, and twelve. Many years later (about seven or eight years ago for me at this point); I became interested in the same thing and began to make notes of the Scriptures that dealt with any number to see where the effort led.

I do not claim to be a prophet or a scholar. In fact I flunked "English" while in school. Much of the contents is lacking correct grammar, actually most of it. I hope the reader can overlook the lack of proper English procedures and wording, and be open to the truth within the context.

As I was documenting the numbers, I began to write a synopsis of each chapter of the Bible, from Genesis to Revelation. I have read the Bible about eight times for this study, and that led to a subject study as well as a number study. The subject of numbers led to a study on prophecy and salvation along with other topics.

I have been asked if recognizing the importance of numbers in the Bible was so important, why had they not been revealed earlier and why these insights had been given to me. I don't know the answer to those questions; all I know is that there seems to be something there, something more, something we have missed in God's Word. If God's Word is truth and we believe all Scripture is inspired by God. Then it is a fact that He recorded in scriptures, certain repeated numbers for a reason. My thought is this. There must be a reason that God would do that, it must be important to Him. Why else would it have been recorded?

This book defines God's purpose for repeating certain numbers continuously but is by no means complete. Every time I read the Word, I discover more numbers of significance, and I hope you do too.

When I began this study, I had no idea where it would lead; it was a beginning without an end. However, as I got to the last few chapters, the unknown became known to me—the message is in the end. It made sense—to understand the message at the end, I had to first understand the beginning, and everything in between.

The Bible is full of symbolism, parables, and events with multiple meanings. The one element that has been missed so often from the scholars is the importance and the significance of the use of numbers in the Bible. God wrote the Word; I just happened to be blessed with discovering greater insight into His Word by discovering the meaning of the numbers He used and revealed. My hope is that the scholar and the common person enjoy it equally.

Introduction

God uses numbers to reveal His ways, His insights, and His wisdom. God declared in the scriptures that His secrets are revealed through His prophets. Prophecies are given to us to inspire our search for Him. To come to know Him, that we will not be taken by surprise, to promote readiness to meet our maker. The purpose of this discovery is to prove God is God, to help us all prepare for His second coming, and to warn others in hopes of saving some.

You will see God is a God of divine order. You will notice some interesting facts and a purposeful plan come together in this study. Some facts may be unpopular and uncomfortable, but even they will allow you to redefine your thinking and deepen your understanding of God. By understanding the numbers in the Word, you will view the Word of God in a new and fascinating way. In studying the numbers in the Bible, you will look in awe of God as the study creates an insight into Him and His wisdom beyond what you could ever imagine or create yourself. A consistent code, if you will, is apparent in His numbering system.

Numbers define the beginning and the end; they help define salvation, direction, creation, hope, mankind and our purpose. Most important, understanding numbers will open the door to understanding the person of Jesus. They define His holiness and righteousness, clarify prophecy, and most of all reveal Him as an awesome God who has a purpose for all that He does. You will discover that each number has a definition; some are the result of the sum, while others are the product of specific numbers. Sometimes the message is just in the numbers.

As my study deepened, I became more and more convinced that the day of the Lord is closer than we think. It is not a comfortable position to take, but it is one I believe to be true. You will find some rather alarming truths not being taught today and others happening now, that are current world events. I wrote this book in hopes of stimulating individual research into the Scriptures, as our lives could depend on it. We are in the day of the Lord! The day of holiness of our God will be revealed and will determine the destiny of every person. It will be a day when all will have to choose the holiness of God or the comfort of man. A day in which the wrath of God falls on all flesh (Jeremiah 45).

The Word of God is unique; one can never stop discovering more truth in it. Every time I read the Word, I discover more. I am sure you too will discover the significance of numbers in the Word of God. It is not mystical—just facts from the

Bible. It does require, however, the opening of your mind, especially in recognizing numbers within numbers. Before passing judgment on what I have written, think outside the box in which we have placed God. I am not a prophet or a great scholar, just someone who wants to reveal the facts, one of which is this: God has a reason for revealing the numbers to us; otherwise, recording them in His Word and to the prophets would not have been important to Him.

As you look at the Scripture references of specific numbers, you may think of some as coincidence. But, are they? I think you will find the consistent revelation of numbers in the Scriptures fascinating.

In this study, you will see that what God has recorded in His Word is not a matter of pure coincidence; it is beyond comprehension and reveals the wholeness of God's creation and plan. Think about it—isn't it true the earth is at a perfect distance from the sun? There are formulas for the purpose of all creation.

Numbers help reveal God's mind, creativity, authority, power, and His plan. This will become apparent as you study *Jesus by Numbers*; numbers do not occur by coincidence, and there is a reason for God's planning and much more yet to be discovered. Understand that there is an abundance of circumstances and usage of numbers and that I have written only a few I have observed. I am sure you will find many more hidden in His Word.

It is important to understand the breakdown and definition of specific numbers as defined by the Scripture references and in each section. In some cases, the Scripture references in bold print support the definition of the numbers. In other cases, the bold print emphasizes the importance of the Scripture.

Have you ever asked yourself why certain numbers are repeated in the Scriptures? What is the significance or the meaning of this? My hope is that once you study this, your perception of the one and only God will change. In seeking to understand the message in the numbers, remember that God has spoken through all time symbolically; His Word contains many parables and metaphors. He does this to challenge those who want to understand and to ask Him for insight into hidden messages, if you will. Even the disciples had to ask for explanations of Jesus' words and stories. His messages were not without meaning and very often are subject to interpretation. We can also apply the same principle in studying the use and repetition of certain numbers found in the Scriptures.

Note that the references pertaining to the use of specific numbers are primarily from the Bible, the original King James Version (about 90%) and the Revised Standard Version (about 9%). About 1% is taken from the "Torah". Sometimes looking beyond what you have a tendency to overlook in casual reading is necessary. Upon completion of this study, you will never overlook God's numbers and take them lightly again.

Right from the beginning in Genesis, seven days, or periods of time, were designated for His creation. Have you ever asked why seven days and not eight or ten, or why this even matters? Or, why it rained for forty days and forty nights for Noah? Why it took forty days for the writing of the Ten Commandments? Why Jesus fasted for forty days, or why upon the resurrection of Jesus- that he stayed and taught for forty days before being taken up in a cloud. Why there will be forty angels used in the judgment of God in the book of Revelation? Why Jesus was crucified on the third hour? Why there were three men crucified, not just one or two? Why Jesus had to remain buried for three days, not some other number of days? Why Noah at the receding of the waters sent out three birds, each seven days apart? Why the numbers three and seven are used continually in the book of Revelation? How about this one, how can God have three attributes, the Father, the Son, and the Holy Spirit and also be composed of seven spirits?

A subtle teaching exists today in the Christian church that pushes us to hunger and thirst after grace instead of righteousness. The truth is that humanity has no fear of God and has lost the holiness of God. In this study, you will learn the wrath and return of God is near due to the sinful condition of people. History does and will repeat itself. The Lord destroyed the earth once and warned He will destroy the earth again. This is because we have exchanged truth for lies.

We are taught that if we follow certain rules, we will be viewed from God as righteous. These rules are sometimes interpreted as a form of imputed righteousness. For example: Some may think because they don't drink alcohol, they are righteous, but that person could be full of coveting or lying. Another example could be to remain married in spite of the fact they are caught up in abusive relationships or perhaps full of anger or jealousy. They continue thinking they are right with God because they remain married while overlooking the less obvious sin, perhaps idolatry, pride or pornography. This to me is imputed righteousness. The church many times looks at the result, not the root. Don't misunderstand me here, I am not supporting divorce or alcohol, but I am saying the judgment of the church needs to be revaluated at times. I use these two as examples only to challenge those in the church whose minds at times remain closed. The discovery of the meaning behind numbers requires an open mind and heart to discover

God even more—especially a concept such as this, which has apparently been overlooked for centuries.

With this, we go into the world of numbers in Scripture. With some numbers, we are told what they represent, while with others, we can figure out their meanings by their patterns of usage, the same way we figure out the meaning of words with multiple meanings. An example of this would be the word *key* with its various definitions: a key to a lock, a keyboard, a key to the heart, a key item, a price key, or a key to understanding. As you will discover, this requires considering all the various definitions and putting them in context.

For the purpose of stimulation of thought, let's use the number three. There are three principles of sin. Three times Noah sent birds out to check for dry land each seven days apart. Three types of animals were required or designated for atonement of sin. Three signs were given to the people of Israel that God had chosen Moses to lead them out of Egypt. Three times a year were designated to celebrate the goodness of God. Moses interceded in prayer three times when God was going to destroy the Israelites because of their sin while in the wilderness for forty years. Balaam made seven altars to the Lord three times. David was given a choice of one of three curses to receive upon himself. Three times Elijah spread himself over a child that had died and the child came back to life. Jonah was in the belly of the great fish for three days and nights. Jesus received three gifts at birth. Satan tempted Jesus after forty days of fasting in three ways. The ministry of Jesus lasted three years. Three disciples witnessed three people, Jesus, Moses, and Elijah, on the Mount of Transfiguration. Peter denied Christ three times. Peter was asked if he loved the Lord three times. Jesus prayed in the garden of Gethsemane three times. Jesus arose from the dead on the third day.

In addition, there are three main entities of God: the Father, the Son, and the Holy Spirit. The sign on the cross-identifying Jesus as the king of the Jews was in three languages. Jesus is described in three time periods - He who was, who is, and who is to come.

Also, note all the sets of three for instruction, correction, and judgment in Scriptures in the pages of Section Three. This should by now stimulate some curiosity as to why is this? The following sections are my attempt to help answer this important why.

This is not written to support a church denomination. It is written that the church would find a common denominator—Jesus.

Section One

The Number One

The number One, represents one God, one savior, one creator, one judge, one king, one redeemer, the holy one, one Lord, the righteous one, one truth, the one Messiah, and the one way, all this in one God with many attributes, the I am. Everything referring to numbers begins with the number one. God is the beginning and the end, the alpha and the omega, and everything in between, all in one. There is no other one. There is only one God, and Jehovah is His name. Even the Father, the Son, and the Holy Spirit are one not just in purpose but also in being. The sum of all His names makes the whole.

- One Lord (Deuteronomy 6, Isaiah 43–49, Mark 12, Romans 2–3, Deuteronomy 6).
- One God (Isaiah 43-49, 60-61, Jeremiah 10, I Corinthians 7-8, I Timothy 2, Mark 12).
- One Savior (Isaiah 43–49, 60–61).
- One Creator (Isaiah 43–49).
- One Judge (Isaiah 33).
- One King (Isaiah 33).
- One Redeemer (Isaiah 43–49, 60–61).
- One Way (John 14).
- Righteous one (Isaiah 45, John 2).
- Holy one (Isaiah 37, 43, Mark 1, 1 John 2, Revelation 2).
- One mediator (1 Timothy 2).
- One salvation (Jeremiah 4).
- One living God (Jeremiah 10).
- Everlasting one (Jeremiah 10).
- One Spirit, one hope, one Lord, one faith, one God (Ephesians 4).
- Mighty one (Isaiah 30, 49).
- When the Lord returns, there will be only one Lord and His name will be "One" (Zechariah 14).
- One God who created man (Malachi 2).
- One Father (Matthew 23).

- One Master (Matthew 23).
- One Christ (Matthew 23).
- The Father, the Son, and the Holy Spirit are one (1 John 5).
- The one living God who is the Savior of all men, especially for those who believe (1 Timothy 4).
- True one (Revelation 3)

Other uses of number "One"

- Jesus was betrayed on the first day of Passover (Matthew 26).
- On the morning of the first day of the week, Jesus arose from the dead (Matthew 28).

Section Two

The Number Two

Two means to bear witness, to confirm an event, or an action to be taken or received from God. We start in Genesis with two angels appearing to Lot to bear witness and proclaim the destruction of Sodom and Gomorrah. Then God used two people to lead the Israelites out of Egypt. Moses was called to lead, but he had a speech problem. God could have healed him, but instead allowed Aaron to serve as Moses' interpreter, so two people led Israel out of the wilderness for forty years. It is interesting that Moses, upon receiving the Ten Commandments from God, smashed the first set. These were written in stone by the hand of God. Later Moses again ascends to the top of the mountain to receive the commandments the second time. It was God's way of demonstrating His Commandments being "confirmed" by Him. The law had to be written twice to bear witness to the author of the law, that being God himself. These commandments were even written on two tablets of stone. Even the stones bore witness to the law.

We see in Ezekiel and in the book of Revelation two witnesses who stand before the throne of God. In the time of the great wrath, these two witnesses will bear the truth for three and a half years about God's grace, love, and judgment before they are finally killed by the antichrist.

In regards to the last days, the Lord extends His arm out to the remnant of Israel twice. This is written to confirm what the prophets have said regarding the destruction of Israel in the last days for mankind.

Early in Jesus' ministry, He sent His disciples two by two to heal the sick, to cast out demons, and to share the good news, bearing witness to Jesus.

One of the most significant accounts of two bearing witness to an event was at the crucifixion of Jesus the Christ. Remember there were three people crucified that day. Jesus hung between two thieves. One was a witness to the actual death and suffering in heaven and the other one was an actual witness of the death of Christ to those in Hell. Both men bore witness first hand. Remember that His legs were not broken; He died just moments before the two who had hung with Him. These two "witnessed and confirmed" the death of Jesus.

Upon the resurrection of Jesus three days later, two angels met Mary at the tomb, both bearing witness to His resurrection.

Jesus spoke throughout the Gospels how He bore witness to the Father and how the Spirit bore witness to Him. However, they both bore witness to the Father. In John, we read **the testimony of two is true**. This statement defines the number and its meaning.

In Revelation 21, the Lord confirmed who He is. He stated the same thing twice for the purpose of confirmation. He is the alpha and the omega, the beginning and the end.

This is not just by accident or mere coincidence, as some may think; it clearly demonstrates that God is a God of order and divine planning in all creation. There is purpose in all He does, even using repeated numbers.

Number Two References

Two of all living creatures were brought into the ark (Genesis 6).

The battle between Ishmael and Isaac is revealed, and how everyone will be against Ishmael who incidentally becomes the father of the Muslims (Genesis 16).

Two angels appear to save Lot and his family from destruction (Genesis 19).

God talks to Abraham the second time about offering Isaac as a sacrifice and identifies Isaac as Abrahams only son (Genesis 22).

Both Abraham and Isaac bore witness to God's opening of their wives' wombs for children (Genesis 21, 25).

Isaac and Rebekah have twin boys. Jacob betrays Esau twice. Esau vows to kill Jacob. These brothers are two nations that will be at war with each other for generations (Genesis 25 & 27).

Joseph and Benjamin were the only sons of Jacob's wife Rachael (Genesis 30).

Joseph interpreted two dreams of famine and feast to come (Genesis 41).

Moses and Aaron performed miracles and the two led the Israelites out of Egypt (Exodus 4 & 6).

Both Joshua and Moses are called to receive the laws of God and both actually saw God (Exodus 24).

The Ten Commandments were written twice, confirming the law (Deuteronomy 9; Exodus 20, 24, 34).

A leper person was to be healed by a priest who used two birds for his cure, killing one and releasing the other (Leviticus 14).

Joshua and Caleb were the only two men that bore witness to the promise to enter the Promised Land. They were the only two witnesses that had faith out of ten, sent as spies. They are the only two out of all Israel that inherit the promise land including Moses. However, Moses did get to see it from a mountaintop. Everyone else over the age of twenty was denied into the promise land due to disobedience to the Lord (Numbers 14 & 32).

The Ten Commandments were written on two tablets of stone (Deuteronomy 4).

Joshua sent two men out as spies into Jericho (Joshua 2).

Gideon set out a fleece twice to get confirmation that the message he was receiving was from God (Judges 6).

The Lord appeared to Samuel twice (1 Samuel 2).

Elijah is awakened by an angel two times and told to eat (1 Kings 19).

The Lord will extend his arm the second time to recover the remnant of Israel (Isaiah 11-12).

The Lord appeared twice to Jeremiah (Jeremiah 33).

Two kingdoms will come together in the last days for a common cause (Daniel 2).

Two dreams were given to king Nebuchadnezzar about the last Babylonian empire (Daniel 1–4).

In reference to the last days, a king from the west side of the world (Daniel 8), destroys the two horns or kings of Media (Iran) and Persia (the Middle East).

There are two spirits of witness before the throne of God. These two will bear witness to the "I am" in the latter days (Zechariah 4).

Two female angels remove the spirit of wickedness (Babylon) until her time to be released (Zechariah 5).

There are two times that a voice from the clouds was heard about Jesus being the son that the Father is well pleased with. The first is at His baptism (Matthew 3). The second time is at the Mount of Transfiguration in Matthew 17. Here the Father "bears witness" to the Son.

On the second day of Passover, the counsel of the chief priests took place and they voted (bore witness) that Jesus must be sentenced to death (Matthew 27).

The disciples were sent out two by two to preach the gospel, heal the sick, and to cast out demons (Mark 6).

Two bore witness to the Christ and His crucifixion. The one thieve bore witness to those in hell and the other thieve bore witness to those in God's kingdom (Luke 23).

John bore witness in two ways to Jesus as the Christ and the Son of God (John 1).

Two angels bore witness to Jesus' resurrection (John 20).

Two conditions must be met in order to see the kingdom of God. You must be born of water and 2) you must be born of the spirit (John 2-3).

The testimony of two is true. Jesus bears testimony to Himself as the Spirit does also. Jesus and God are the same "I am" (John 8).

Jesus wrote in the ground twice when a woman was accused of committing adultery and then He told her to sin no more (John 8). I believe he wrote the names of those casting the stones in the ground. He was bearing witness to their sin by writing twice in the sand.

Jesus, the second of the Trinity, bears witness to the Father, and the Holy Spirit bears witness to the Son (John 5).

Two witnesses stand before the throne of God; they are identified as two olive trees, symbolic of being of Jewish heritage. These two witnesses will be given power to prophecy and perform miracles in the latter days in Jerusalem. I think they are the same witnesses that were at the Mount of Transfiguration, Elijah and Moses (Mark 9). They will lay dead for three and one half days for the world to view before they are resurrected. There will be a great earthquake at that time and a tenth of the city is destroyed and 7,000 people are killed (Revelation 11).

Two leaders will arise in the last days: the false prophet and the antichrist (Revelation 13).

Two evil spirits will be removed from earth, Death and Hades. A second death falls on those not following Christ, and are thrown into the lake of fire (Revelation 20).

Two attributes describe the eternal God: the alpha, the omega, the beginning, and the end—a confirmation (Revelation 21). Note the two sets of two.

Two items for life are found in the New Jerusalem: the River of Life and the Tree of Life (Revelation 22).

Section Three

The Number Three

The number three represents perfection, consecration, and or purification.
It is one of the most significant numbers repeated throughout Scriptures. Not only
does it represent God, it sometimes reflects God working through a man. It can also
reveal God working through circumstances or events to purify or make perfect. It
also represents someone or something consecrated to God.

Those who study the number three in Scripture will see an obvious pattern
when they look at the person or the event-taking place. Again, the event often
reflects God's perfection or His working in the event or person with His stamp of
perfection or consecration. When Noah was in the ark for 40 days and nights of
rain and then after 150 days of floating on the water, he was led to send birds out to
find dry land. The first bird returned; this indicated there was no dry land. Seven
days later, he sent out the second bird, which returned with a leaf. After another
seven days he sent out a third bird that did not return. This was a sign to Noah that
dry land was appearing, that God's judgment upon the earth had been perfected,
and that the earth was once again consecrated to the Lord along with Noah and
the seven people with him to make eight. Eight means "set apart," in this case, from
the rest of the world. Seven as we will see, means "complete." In this passage, three
and seven symbolize the "perfect and complete" judgment on mankind.

Moses received three signs to confirm he was the one chosen to lead the
Israelites out of Egypt. The first was his staff when he threw it down turned into
a snake. The second being that he suddenly had leprosy on his hand and the third,
was when the staff was used to turn the waters of the Nile River like blood.

God established that there would be three times a year the Israelites were
to celebrate His goodness, the law, and to seek forgiveness for their sin. These
are still celebrated today after thousands of years within their culture. The first
being Passover which commemorates God's goodness of not bringing death on
the firstborn of the Jews while in Egypt. The second is the Feast of Weeks, and the
third is the Feast of Tabernacles.

The law given to Moses specified three kinds of animals for a sin offering for
the people. Not only were there only three acceptable types of animals, but they

had to be at least seven days old and without blemish. They had to be perfect, just as later, the sin offering for all humanity, Jesus, also had to be perfect.

Only three items were designated as a cereal offering of holiness, and three requirements for a sheath offering. There were three requirements for each type of offering, and there were to be three offerings per year.

Three commands were given to the people by Moses, that they would be made perfect and consecrated to God: they were to worship God Jehovah only and to love Him with all their 1) mind and 2) soul, and 3) to seek Him with all of their heart. If they were to keep these three conditions, everything would go well with them.

Regarding the day of wrath of the Lord, three woes are mentioned twice in the Scriptures or "confirmed," if you will, in the Old Testament in Isaiah and in the New Testament in Revelation. One of the woes is so bad that all heaven will be silent for about thirty minutes before its execution.

Another sign confirmed (twice) in Isaiah and in Revelation is in the mention of the angels singing "Holy, holy, holy." Why was this not mentioned just once? Once should have been enough. However, if you look at it under the perspective of the significance of numbers, it declares "perfect holiness" by mentioning it three times. This somehow fits in praising God. The fact that it was mentioned twice, in Isaiah and Revelation, "confirms His perfect holiness."

We are told that all of mankind should fear God, the one who determines our eternity of eternal joy or eternal damnation. We are to fear Him for three reasons: 1) He is the true, one, and only God, 2) He is the living God and 3) He is the everlasting and eternal God.

Many have asked why the Israelites were chosen to be God's people. It is simply that He chose them to be an example to other nations, to demonstrate what happens to a people if they obey or disobey God. Interestingly enough He chose them for three reasons: First He chose them to be a name. Then they were chosen as a representative, a witness of Jehovah. Thirdly, He chose them to be a glory. Even though they were chosen, they do not listen to God. Therefore, He has to punish them to make an example out of them to all the nations.

The wrath of God that comes upon the earth and mankind in the end is due to three sins. The first is that we have forgotten God. The second is that men follow other gods and the third is that mankind serve themselves (Jeremiah 16). This is an important declaration for us to recognize and understand. We have forgotten the one and only true God and we claim we do not need Him except when we are in trouble or despair. Think of all the gods we worship: our favorite athletes and celebrities, our cars and jobs, food and music, money, politics, even our children—the list goes on. We even make doing our own thing and being self-indulgent into a god. Where we put our mind, soul and heart becomes our God. The three sins are a definition of our wretchedness as "perfect sin in man."

Nebuchadnezzar sought an interpretation to a dream; he had two confirmed dreams pertaining to the end of time. He sought an interpretation three times, and on the third time, Daniel told him the dream he had and interpreted it. The dream had been sent to warn people of the latter days so they would not be caught by surprise. Scriptures declared that this message for the last days was to be given so man would understand. It was a perfect interpretation of what was to come.

Jonah was called to be an evangelist to Nineveh, but he did not want to do what God had called him to do. He tried to run from God; he boarded a ship going the opposite direction. Then a great storm came, it was discovered that the storm was due to Jonah's running from God. He was thrown overboard and swallowed by a great fish. Some might say this was gross, but it was God's way of providing Jonah a safe, although not to pleasant, passage to dry land. He was in the belly of the fish for three days and three nights. Even Jesus confirmed He had to be in the center of the earth for three days to be perfected. Jonah ended up preaching for forty days in Nineveh. The people in Nineveh turned back to God as a result of Jonah's teaching.

After His baptism, Jesus went into the woods fasting and praying for forty days and nights. At the end of the forty days, Satan came to Jesus and tempted Him in three ways. The first temptation was food, a necessity for life, especially for one without food for so long. The second temptation was to test God. Satan also tempted Jesus the third time by offering power over all the domain of earth. If one were to study these events, it would be noted that Satan even used the scriptures or truth if you will, to tempt Jesus. However, they were scriptures that were taken out of context and twisted to tempt Jesus in an effort to betray him. Then note that Satan left him after three temptations to wait for another perfect opportunity. That I believe, was upon the crucifixion, the last "perfect temptation" during the last three hours Jesus suffered on the cross.

The number three throughout the Bible is always in reference to perfection. It depicts a person, thing, or event that is perfect and consecrated to the Lord. It can also mean to purify or make pure or perfect. Jesus said He had to die, be buried, and rise on the third day in order to be perfected.

One of the most significant uses of the number three is found during the death of Jesus. Let's look at the facts and be sure to pay attention to all the three's. Just before being betrayed, Jesus was with three disciples in the garden of Gethsemane, and He prayed three times. Jesus was betrayed on the first day of Passover, a period of seven days for purification and reflection for the Jews. On the second day of Passover, He was judged guilty by the Jewish counsel; they bore "witness" against Him on the second day. He was crucified between two others, who witnessed His death. Our Savior had two witnesses; one went to hell and the other witness went to heaven, note three people were crucified on that day, One Savior with two witnesses.

Here is an example of the first lesson of noticing numbers within numbers. Jesus was hung on the cross at three in the afternoon, the third hour. Three hours later, the sixth hour everything is darkened. Three hours later at the ninth hour, Jesus dies for a total of six hours that He hung upon the cross. If you notice the pattern here, you will see two distinct sets of three-hour periods. Remember that the number two signifies confirmation or bearing witness to something. Here is a little insight into what comes later in recognizing "sets of numbers." If you break the number six down as recorded in the passage it would be like this. Two times three equals six, which would be translated as "confirmed perfection of a man." This of course is in reference to what Christ achieved in His crucifixion, but more on this later. Understand that the number six, (six hours) represents man; thus even in His crucifixion, the numbers symbolized His death "was for man". Then remember He arose from the dead on the third day. Jesus stated He had to die and rise from the grave on the third day in order to be perfected. Accidental? I think not.

Even if you do not agree with what I am saying, you have to admit there is something peculiar about the usage of specific numbers throughout Scripture. In this major event, you can see the symbolism demonstrated concerning His death, a message within the message, if you will.

Remember when Satan accuses Job of only being a righteous man because of God's presence is with Job. Satan is then given permission from God to do what he wanted to do to Job except take his life. Job subsequently went through a period without the presence of God in his life. This was the ultimate test for Job. The feeling of abandonment from God the Father.

I believe that when the sky turned dark at the crucifixion of Jesus, that is, the second half of the six hours, the last three hours, Satan went to God the Father and accused Jesus. Scripture teaches that the accuser stands before the throne of God constantly accusing the righteous. His accusation was that Jesus was able to die for the world only because of the Father's presence was upon him. I believe that Satan stated, "Remove your [the Father's] presence and he will curse you."

At that point, the presence of God the Father was removed from Jesus, and in those last three hours, the sky was darkened. **He was tested and perfected as only a man**. He was tempted as a man as He hung there and questioned God the Father for three hours. He was made perfect by defeating Satan's perfect temptation, feeling abandoned by God. You could look at it as, "Perfect timing."

Toward the end of this three hour period, Jesus expressed to God the Father, "Why have you left me?" This revealed His agony, torment, and abandonment He was experiencing. It was not only a moment during which the Father turned away from Jesus because of all the sin of humanity on Him. It was also Jesus in agony without the Father's presence. We were given a clue, which was revealed by the darkness that overcame the land for three hours.

During that three-hour period, God the Father turned His eyes away from Jesus. Jesus cried out with His soul full of pain and suffering as a man without the presence of God for three hours, the "perfect temptation." Think about it; if the presence of God had guided Jesus throughout His life, the ultimate test would have been the loss of the Fathers' presence, even losing sight of His purpose. To suffer for people who didn't care about what He was doing. It had to be a perfect temptation, a perfect opportunity for Jesus to act in the flesh, especially out of anger or revenge.

Remember when Jesus was tempted after forty days and Satan left him waiting for another opportunity. The last three hours Jesus hung on the cross was Satan's "perfect" opportunity for the last temptation that Jesus had to overcome. The feeling of being abandoned by God, being left in His own human strength. Personally, I cannot think of a more perfect temptation to overcome than knowing you are doing the will of the Father but feeling abandoned by Him, especially for the last three hours of agony in His life. This temptation was made perfect and confirmed, or bore witness to at the same time by the two thieves that hung with him. Do you think this is a possibility?

Some other insights on three representing perfection or consecration come in recognizing believers in Christ. Scriptures teach that there are three ways to recognize believers: by their goodness, their righteousness, and their witness to the truth.

Three results come from the testing of our faith: steadfastness, perfection, and completion. We are tested to be made perfect in three ways. Another very important understanding is that God is one composed of three attributes: the Father, the Son, and the Holy Spirit. Many Christians have a hard time understanding this. Perhaps these simple illustrations will help.

If you look at an Orange in its complete form, it can be described by its peel, its pulp, and its juice. You can also describe an orange as a fruit, by its color, as a sphere, as being round, or even like a ball. Note the characteristics described by different words all refer to the same thing. That is how it is with God. Now let's dissect this. If we remove the peel, is it a complete orange, or do we see just a different part of the orange? Is the peel when separated, an Orange of itself? Is it a separate Orange or a part simply separated from the whole? Some try to separate Jesus from being God. They explain that Jesus becomes a separate god, instead of realizing he is a piece, separated from the whole. Now let's go one-step further, what if you separated the juice and the pulp. Is it still an Orange or are you seeing the different combined elements that make the parts of the whole? Without all the peeling, the juice and the pulp coming together as designed, you have three components of an orange, but no longer a whole orange. It is the sum of the parts that makes the whole.

This also is true with God; you can separate God's components, but they are still God, just not in His truest form. He is seen as perfect only as three in one—the peel, the juice, and the pulp, the Father, the Son, and the Holy Spirit. Again, the sum of the three parts makes the whole.

Another example would be if we broke down water, a necessity for all life. Do you see the symbolism of water as a life requirement made of three components, just as God is a basic need in our lives, also made of three components? In fact, He is the River of life. Our bodies are mostly water. Water can take three forms: gas, liquid, or a solid. Water has two elements, Hydrogen and Oxygen. If put together as designed, it becomes water. Again, the sum makes the whole. It is interesting that within the formula for water, we have another key element for life, Oxygen. See the symbolism of God breathing life, the breath of life, into Adam? Without these three components combined, we do not have water. Without Oxygen, we would not be able to breathe nor would we have water. Put this in context with understanding the Father, the Son, and the Holy Spirit. Combined, they make God; separately, they are elements of God. This is the design of God in His truest form. We cannot help recognize throughout nature the revealing of His divine plan. The Creator has created nature, water in this case, to bear witness to Himself, and to call us to Him. God tells us He also bears witness to Himself in three ways: through signs, through wonders, and through miracles.

Until Jesus returns, He will be recognized in three ways, He who was, who is, and who is to come. When He returns, He will bear three names: the Word of God, the King of kings, and the Lord of lords. He will actually have the last two of these three names inscribed on his body bearing witness to the first name, the Word of God.

Next, let's look at the use of number three in Revelation where it is continuously repeated and symbolic at the same time. Take note that the purpose of the first three chapters of Revelation is to warn the believers in the end times to repent, to be right with God and to encourage those already obeying him. One must recognize that you must use the original King James Bible translation to understand the information regarding numbers. The lack of recognizing that numbers are significant, has been overlooked and misinterpreted some times. In this passage, it is necessary to take note of the sets of three, within addressing the seven churches. In the first three chapters, using different terminology, Jesus claims to be the alpha and the omega three times, this is the first set. The second of three sets, states that He was, He is and He is to come, which is mentioned twice (confirmed). The next four sets of three is to four of the churches. Jesus identifies himself to each of the four in three ways. In the last set of three He is the living one, was dead, and is now alive. **His qualifications for judgment are described seven times to the churches, each time with three qualifications.** We also see His physical appearance described in ten ways, which represents "holiness." If you include His clothing in His description, He is described in twelve ways, which represents "authority." Combined, these parts make the whole or "holiness with authority." This fits the context as to why Jesus explains His authority in the final judgment upon humanity in Revelation.

The four churches are told to repent or receive the penalty thereof. There are four churches in which Jesus claims His authority is to be recognized, each having three ways. Each of the four contains three characteristics revealing the person of Jesus. The first is that, He is the first and the last, who died, but is now alive. The second set is, He is the word of God, having eyes like fire, and feet like bronze. The third set that again identifies Jesus is that He is the word of the Holy one, the True one and has the key of David. The fourth set being, from the words of the Amen, the faithful true witness, the beginning of God's creation. If you took the product of the four churches, times three descriptions of Jesus given to each of the four, you once again get twelve total descriptions of the authority of Christ. Incidentally twelve is the number that represents "authority". Jesus is revealing His authority again to the churches through the numbers. If we took three times four equals twelve, it would be translated as, He is the "perfect judge with authority." This is the second time in the message to the churches that He describes his qualifications by using sets of three. The first was seven sets of three; the second time is within the first set of four sets of three. It is interesting that four churches are told to repent, and three are recognized as the "perfect church" and are told to remain faithful, and persevere to the end.

These sets are given, so the church would understand without a doubt as to whom the author of the salutations to the churches is, and by whose authority. Can you see the significance of the number three referring to one that is perfect or consecrated to God? Also, note there are actually seven separate sets of three (with one set repeated to make eight), descriptions of Jesus when He is identifying himself to the believers or the churches, within the first three chapters of Revelation. As we continue the study on numbers, it will be important to remember and recognize the use of the numbers four, five, seven, eight and twelve in this passage of Revelation. I am getting ahead of myself here a bit, but for reference purposes, please note. In the first seven sets of three, if you were to put this into a formula as three (perfect) plus seven (complete) equals ten (holiness), you end up with Jesus identifying His qualifications to the church as one that is "perfectly complete in holiness."

The last few chapters of Revelation include interesting facts about three. Jesus stated that the angel sent to testify to the information given to John was to be given to the churches. Then He identified Himself again with three factors of recognition: The first was that He was the root, second as the offspring of David, and third that He was the bright morning star. This is the second passage of time in which He uses sets of three explanations, "confirming" His qualifications and authority to the church. The first is in the first three chapters of Revelation and the second in chapter 21 and 22. The request for Jesus to come is mentioned three times: the first being from the Spirit and the bride (the church) saying, "Come." The second is from him who hears says, "Come," and the third is he who is thirsty says, "Come." Within the context, Jesus promises three times He will come quickly. Here we have another set of three with three responses in each set at the return of Jesus in the last book of Revelation. It is another example of three sets of three at the end of the world, the omega. He also describes His servants with a set of three, stating they will worship him, they will see His face, and third that His name will be on their foreheads.

The first three chapters of Revelation reveal the beginning of the end, and the last chapter is the end of the end, the omega. In this last chapter of the Bible, Jesus revealed His authority, His identification, if you will, with three truths about himself. Then there are three invitations for His return. He claims three times that indeed He will return. This is to be understood as a "perfect promise." Again three sets of three, each with three points. If we put this in a number format, it would be 333. The usage and repeating of number three reveals the symbolism and represents a "perfect God with a perfect plan with a perfect ending." The numbers fit. Another important factor not to miss in Revelation 22 is that there are four sets of three representing "Jesus as the perfect judge". Two sets describe Jesus and two sets confirm His return. I am jumping ahead of myself here but to start your thinking process, please consider this. Number four represents "judgment." Another way to break this down would be three times four, which equals twelve; translated as "the perfect judge with authority." What better way to represent Jesus within the numbers used. As the Jews say, "it is the sum that makes the whole" regarding numbers.

Compare the numbers of describing Jesus to the counterfeit, the antichrist is interestingly enough identified with a set of three sixes, 666; He is also identified with six sets. Within each set, there are three definitions of the antichrist in Revelation. In addition, note how the antichrist will try to counterfeit the true Christ in three ways.

The first set of six is the beast being described three times as having seven heads and seven crowns (seven means completion). Compare this to the slain Lamb before the throne of God having seven horns and seven eyes.

In the second set of three, the beast is described with three attributes: as cunning as a leopard, as powerful as a bear, and as a hungry devouring lion. The third set described what the dragon will give the beast: his power, his seat, and his great authority. Compare this to what is given to Jesus-honor, glory and power. In the fourth set of three, we see three demonic frogs coming out of three mouths, those of the dragon, the beast, and the false prophet.

In the fifth set, we see three additional counterfeits of Satan; he was, is not, and is to come, only to descend to the bottomless pit. The sixth set is a repeat of the fifth set stated in Revelation 17 and is repeated in chapter 20, a "confirmation." This is a reflection of number two we studied earlier that confirms or emphasizes the point that the antichrist was, is not, and is to come only to descend to the bottomless pit. Incidentally, "six represents man and or imperfection" (see "The Number Six"). To sum it up we have six sets, each composed of three descriptions of the antichrist and the imperfect, thus the number 666, "the imperfect man described perfectly."

We also discover in Revelation three sets of three describing heaven with which a new heaven and earth are described: a New Jerusalem and a new temple, where God will dwell with mankind. The first set offers three new descriptions of eternal life: no death, no tears, and no pain. The second set of three describes the city in three ways: with walls of Jasper, a city of gold and transparent. In the third set, we are told three things will remain eternal: there will be no need for light, for He will be the light; the glory of the Lord will fill the city; and there will be no evil, only His righteousness (Revelation 21).

There are a set of three gates, each set is facing four directions with three angels at each gate. There are twelve foundations to the wall. The foundations are adorned with twelve types of precious stones with three new names of each of the disciples at each gate. The twelve gates are like twelve pearls.

Scriptures teach that Jesus is in the process of "perfecting" the saints, those who believe and follow Him. Many qualifications or definitions of believers are in sets of three. One of the first sets is to baptize in the name of the Father, the Son, and the Holy Spirit. There are three teachings on prayer: to seek, to knock, and to ask. **Three conditions are required of believers: they must love the Lord with all their heart, their mind, and their soul.** We are to abide in faith, hope, and love. All believers have to be steadfast, immovable, and abounding in His work. Followers of Christ are to be kind, tenderhearted, and forgiving. Believers can be recognized in three ways: by their goodness, their righteousness, and their truth. Believers are not to be involved in fornication, impurity, or coveting. If we are to follow Jesus, we must let the peace of Christ rule our hearts, be thankful, and let the Word dwell in us richly.

Another set of three commands given to believers involves being steadfast in prayer, being watchful, and being thankful to fulfill the ministry the Lord has given us. True believers have 1) pure hearts, 2) good consciences, and 3) sincere faith.

The Lord gives believers a spirit of power, a spirit of love, and a spirit of self-control. We are told to rejoice in the Lord always, to have no anxiety about anything but in three things—prayer, supplication, and thanksgiving—let our requests be known to Him.

The three results we can expect from tests of our faith are steadfastness, perfection, and completion. The three principles of real faith are being quick to listen, being slow to speak, and being slow to anger. Above all, we are to recognize the three principles of truth: God is truth, He who abides in love abides in God, and God will abide in him.

Do you think it to be interesting on how God is in the business of perfecting us with so many sets of perfection? He demonstrates the importance by using a repeat of the number meaning "perfection," the number three.

As you study the references below, you will see that many of the godly attributes we are to seek are designated with three qualities. Also notice the sets of three repeatedly used. You will notice these are Godly or perfect qualities we are to seek in sets of three, if we are to be made perfect in Christ. The most important set is that we are to love the Lord with all our 1) mind, 2) heart, 3) and soul.

Number Three References

From the beginning, there have been three principles of sin: temptation, the act, and the lack of accountability or to blame someone else (Genesis 3).

Three times Noah sent birds out to seek dry land- these were each seven days apart (Genesis 8).

Three types of animal life are required for atonement of sin (Genesis 15).

Three descriptions of Noah are mentioned: his righteousness, he was blameless, and he walked with God (Genesis 16).

Three men appear to Abraham to inform him that he would have a son, and that they had come to destroy Sodom and Gomorrah (Genesis 18).

Joseph put his brothers in jail for three days (Genesis 42–43).

Moses was three months old when placed in a basket in the Nile (Exodus 2).

God is the God of three patriots, Abraham, Isaac and Jacob (Exodus 3).

Three signs were given to the Israelites to prove God had chosen Moses to lead them out of Egypt (Exodus 4).

Three days of darkness came over Egypt (Exodus 10).

The Israelites were to consecrate themselves for three days (Exodus 19).

Three times a year the Israelites were to celebrate God's goodness (Exodus 23).

Moses performed three sets of forty in delivering the Ten Commandments. The first time he received the Commandments, they were written in forty days, but he broke them. The Lord wanted to destroy the people, but Moses interceded with prayer for forty days. Moses went back a second time for another forty days to have the Lord rewrite the Commandments, "confirming them." Moses fasted for each of those forty-day periods (Deuteronomy 9; Exodus 24 and 34). Here is a little insight: three times forty equals a hundred and twenty, symbolic of "perfect judgment by holiness that equals holiness with authority," more on this later.

Three types of creatures were required as atonement for sin by burnt offerings (Leviticus 1).

Three items were used for a cereal offering of holiness (Leviticus 2).

When the Israelites were to come into the Promised Land, they were to wait three years to eat any fruit they had planted to allow time for the fruit to become holy (Leviticus 19).

It is given that the sprinkling of blood on three locations- the veil, the altar, and the mercy seat -had to be done seven times for the forgiveness of sin (Leviticus 4, 8, and 6).

Three requirements for a sheaf offering (Leviticus 23).

Three leaders who rebelled against Moses were swallowed up along with their families by the ground and went to hell (Numbers 16).

Three times Moses interceded with prayer that God would not destroy the people (Exodus 34; Numbers 14, 16; Deuteronomy 9).

The requirements for being clean were to be celebrated on the third day (Numbers 19).

A donkey spoke to Balaam after being struck by him three times (Numbers 22).

Three times Balaam made seven altars to the Lord; He blessed Israel three times (Numbers 23–24).

Moses chose men to help in the leadership of the people with three qualifications: wisdom, understanding, and experience (Deuteronomy 1).

Three commands of the law: love the Lord your God with all your heart, with all your soul, and with all your might (Deuteronomy 6).

God will love you, bless you, and multiply you for your obedience (Deuteronomy 7).

Three commands given that things may go well with you (Deuteronomy 11).

Three designated yearly celebrations: Passover, the Feast of Weeks, and the Feast of Tabernacles (Deuteronomy 16).

Three times yearly, the Israelites were to eat unleavened bread (Deuteronomy 16).

God declared or chose Israel with three sets, each set with three ways: 1) with affliction, 2) with toil, and 3) with oppression. He brought them out of

Egypt with 1) a mighty hand, 2) a great terror and 3) with signs and wonders. He chose them to be 1) His possession, 2) to make them an example, and 3) to be praise unto the Lord (Deuteronomy 26).

Saul, selected by the Lord, arrived in a town after looking for his father's three donkeys for three days (1 Samuel 9).

Saul met three men on his journey home to confirm his being the future king (1 Samuel 10).

An evil spirit took over Saul three times (1 Samuel 16, 18, 19).

David is fearful of his life and requests a favor from Jonathan. David hides for three days. At the end of three days, Jonathan is to shoot three arrows as a signal to David if it was safe for him. After Jonathan did so, David bowed on the ground to Jonathan three times (1 Samuel 20).

David had three opportunities to kill Saul yet spared his life (1 Samuel 19, 24, 26, 29).

David had three wives. Bathsheba was his third wife (1 Samuel 30, 2 Samuel 11).

David had to choose one of three curses to accept upon himself (2 Samuel 12).

David in his pride ordered a census. The prophet Gad went to David and convicted him. God gave him three choices of punishment: seven years of famine, three months of being pursued by the enemy, or three days of pestilence in the land. David chose the pestilence, and 70,000 people died in three days (2 Samuel 24, 1 Chronicles 21).

Solomon was given three blessings in life (1 Kings 3).

Elijah stretched over a dead boy three times to bring him back to life (1 Kings 17).

God reminded Elijah with three signs confirming who He is (1 Kings 19).

Three times, fifty men were sent to destroy Elijah (2 Kings 2).

When the Lord prepared Elijah to be taken up to heaven, Elijah asked Elisha not to go with him three times. Elisha refused to leave him. After the third time Elijah asks Elisha what he would like in return. Elisha asks for a double portion of Elijah's spirit. A chariot of fire separates them and Elijah is taken to heaven. Elisha was told by prophets three times that Elijah would be taken away that day. Elisha gave permission to look for Elijah's body for three days (2 Kings 2).

Three woes are given regarding the judgment by God on the earth (Isaiah 5, Revelation 8).

Angels in heaven sing "Holy, holy, holy" three times, representing perfect holiness. The fact that this is mentioned twice "confirms it" (Isaiah 6, Revelation 4).

After the three woes upon Israel in the last days, only 10% (a remnant) of the people are left (Isaiah 6).

A set of three definitions of God are given, He is our judge, our lawgiver, and our king (Isaiah 33).

The wisdom and knowledge of God provide stability, strength, and salvation (Isaiah 33).

God remembered three things about Israel (Jeremiah 2).

The Lord lives by three ways, truth, judgment, and righteousness (Jeremiah 4).

God tells man not to be caught up in three glory's, 1) wisdom, 2) might, or 3) riches. But to know God as a God who practices, 1) steadfast love, 2) judgment, and 3) righteousness (Jeremiah 9).

All humanity should fear God, for He is the true God, the living God, and the everlasting God (Jeremiah 10).

The Lord chose Israel to be, 1) a name, 2) a praise and 3) a glory to Him- but they did not listen (Jeremiah 13).

He will destroy Israel because of disobedience in three ways, by sword, by famine, and by pestilence (Jeremiah 14).

Three things God removes from His people because of their sin: love, peace, and mercy (Jeremiah 16).

Because of three sins—forgetting God, following other gods, and selfishness—the wrath of God must come upon the world (Jeremiah 16).

During affliction, we are to remember that God is our strength, our fortress, and our refuge (Jeremiah 16).

Three forms of punishment for sin will come on Israel in the last days, war, famine, and pestilence (Jeremiah 29).

Three qualities about His judgment will exist when His wrath is poured out on man. God will judge us according to our ways, punish us for our sin, and show us no mercy (Ezekiel 7).

God is the God of three patriots, the God of Abraham, Isaac and Jacob (Exodus 3).

God is upset with man because 1) he has no truth, 2) no mercy, and 3) no knowledge of God (Hosea 4).

Nebuchadnezzar sought an interpretation of his dream, which Daniel gives him on the third time. Daniel not only interprets the dream but describes the dream also. Daniel clarifies that his God is in charge of all who rule and who do not rule kingdoms (Daniel 4).

Three men were thrown into the furnace because of their faith in God (Daniel 3).

Daniel prayed three times a day (Daniel 6).

Daniel fasted and prayed for three weeks to understand the message given to Jeremiah. This incidentally is to be understood as, three times seven days. Do you see the message hidden within the numbers? Three symbolizes perfection, and seven represents completion. God gave Daniel a "perfect and complete understanding" of what Jeremiah had prophesied (Daniel 10).

Hosea has three children which the Lord names. Each name represents Gods rejection and anger toward Israel because of their pollution (Hosea 1).

Jonah was in the whale for three days and nights (Jonah 2).

The Lord states that for even three transgressions of eight cities, He will not turn away from punishing them (Amos 1 & 2).

There are three righteous characteristics of God, He is a jealous God, He seeks revenge, and He brings wrath (Nahum 1-3).

God will build the third and last temple (the perfect temple) upon his return (Zechariah 6). Take note this happens at the end of the seven-year tribulation. Now it is not only the perfect temple, but also the "complete and pure Temple." The third and last temple in which God will enter from the East gate and dwell in is described in Ezekiel 40-43.

Jesus received three gifts from most likely three wise men (Matthew 1–2).

Three times Jesus was referred to as a resident of different places: He was recognized as being, from Nazareth of Galilee, from Bethlehem of Judah and called out of Egypt (Matthew 2).

Satan tempted Jesus three times after forty days of fasting and prayer. Jesus responded with three references from the Word to live by- God's Word is the source of life, do not tempt God, and worship and serve God only and no other god (Matthew 4, Luke 4).

Jesus foretold His sign of being in the center of the earth for three days and nights (Matthew 12).

Jesus began His ministry at the age of thirty, which lasted three years and was crucified at age thirty-three. I am a little ahead of myself, but here is a little insight of further understanding and the direction I am headed. When specific numbers are given, we can make a formula that can then be interpreted. In this case take three times ten, plus three, equals thirty-three, Translation: Jesus is "perfect holiness made perfect." By the way, number ten means "holiness".

Three disciples saw the transfiguration of Jesus, Moses and Elijah (Matthew 17).

Peter denied Christ three times (Matthew 26). Why specifically three times?

Jesus prayed three times in the garden of Gethsemane (Matthew 26, Mark 14).

Jesus rose from the dead on the third day to be perfected (Matthew 28; Luke 13, 24).

We are given directions to baptize in the name of the Father, the Son, and the Holy Spirit (Matthew 28).

Three men were crucified (Mark 15).

Three teachings on prayer: seek, knock, and ask (Luke 11).

Jesus was crucified at the third hour (Mark 14, 15). He was on the cross until the ninth hour, a total of six hours. Darkness occurred from the sixth to the ninth hour or the second set of three hours (Matthew 27, Luke 23). This is a case of numbers within numbers, by two sets of three being recognized.

There is also within the message of the crucifixion another message with the number three: We first notice three people being crucified or the "perfect" death. Breaking it down further, we notice two witnesses of the death of Jesus, one to those in hell and one to those in heaven. This fulfills the Law of Moses that one could not be put to death without two witnesses. Next add number one or "Savior." The sum equals three, in a math form (2+1=3), reflecting "two witnesses of the "one" Savior resulting in a perfect death"

There are three conditions that reflect our love for the Lord; we are to love him with all our mind, heart, and soul (Luke 12).

Three facts about the Word of God, the word existed in the beginning, the word was God and the word became flesh and dwelt among us (John 1).

When the word became flesh, three eternal attributes were given to Him, grace, truth and glory (John 1).

Jesus proclaimed three truths, that He is the way, the truth and the life. The only way into the kingdom of God is through Him (John 14).

Jesus asked Peter three times if he loved Him (John 21).

The sign on Jesus' cross read, "King of the Jews" which was written in three languages (John 18–19).

Paul was blind for three days (Acts 9).

Peter has a vision of a sheet held up by the four corners of the earth three times (Acts 10).

Three miracles helped Peter escape from prison (Acts 12).

Paul waited three years before commencing preaching; this shows he had to be perfected, consecrated first.

We will have tribulations and trials; however, they produce three things, patience, experience and hope (Romans 5).

"Faith, hope and love, these three we are to abide in, the greatest being love" (1 Corinthians 12–13).

There are three goals to seek, to be steadfast, to be immovable and be abounding in God's work (1 Corinthians 15).

Paul asked the Lord three times to be delivered of his thorn in his flesh (2 Corinthians 14).

God is the author of 1) wisdom, 2) knowledge, and 3) enlightenment, which gives hope and power to those that believe (Ephesians 1).

As followers of Christ we are to pursue three things, be kind to one another, tenderhearted, and forgiving one another (Ephesians 4).

There are three ways to recognize a true believer by- his goodness, his righteousness and his truth (Ephesians 5).

There are three things that are not to be found in believers, fornication, impurity, and coveting (Ephesians 5).

Jesus' followers are to let the peace of Christ rule their hearts, be thankful, and let the Word dwell in them richly (Colossians 3).

We are to be steadfast in prayer, be watchful, and be thankful. We are to fulfill the ministry, which we have received from the Lord (Colossians 4).

Believers are to seek pure hearts, good consciences, and sincere faith (1 Timothy 1).

The Lord gives us a spirit of power, a spirit of love, and a spirit of self-control (2 Timothy 1–2).

We are to rejoice in the Lord always. To have no anxiety about anything, but in prayer, supplication, and thanksgiving let our requests be made known to Him (Philippians 4).

God bears witness to Himself by signs, wonders, and miracles (Hebrews 1–2).

There are three results of temptation and our sinful nature, 1) we are tempted, 2) to act on it and 3) it brings death (James 1). You can also compare this with the sin of Adam and Eve in Genesis.

When tested in our faith, we receive three results, steadfastness, perfection, and completion (James 1).

Believers are to be quick to listen, slow to speak, and slow to anger (James 1).

There are also three natural sins: lust of the flesh, lust of the eyes, and the pride of life (1 John 2).

Three principles of truth: God is truth, he who abides in love abides in God, and God will abide in him (1 John 4).

There are three witnesses to Jesus, the Spirit, the water, and the blood, and these three agree (1 John 5).

We are given three commands to keep in the latter days, pray constantly, love God, and wait for the Lord with perseverance (Jude).

Jesus is described in three periods of eternal time, who was, who is, and who is to come (Revelation 1).

The Lord speaks directly to those that claim to be following Him in the last days. The first three chapters of Revelation are meant to be a warning to those that believe. It is important to understand that seven churches existed at the time Revelation was written. However, they symbolically represent the churches or believers in the end times.

Jesus identifies himself to four churches, each with a set of three qualifications for His judgment. To Smyrna, the first set is, He is the first and the last, died, and He now lives. To the church of Thyatira, His Words are of the Son of God, with eyes like a flame of fire, and His feet are like bronze. To the church of Philadelphia, He has the words of the holy one, He is the true one, and He has the keys of David. To the fourth church- Laodicea, He is identified with a set of three qualifications. The first is that He is the words of the Amen; He is the faithful and true witness, the beginning of God's creation (Revelation 2-3). If we took the product of the four churches each with three qualifications, we end up with twelve, which incidentally, represents "authority." The Lord is confirming and revealing the message within the message to the churches of His "authority" to judge the world including the church.

Note there are six churches each recognized by a set of three traits each being different. The church of Ephesus is recognized for their works, their toil and their endurance. The church of Smyrna is recognized with three qualities, their tribulation, their poverty, and their blasphemy by declaring they were believers but were actually of Satan. Pergamum, dwells with Satan, they sacrifice to idols, and practice immorality. The church of Sardis is recognized for their works, for being alive, but they are dead. The church of Philadelphia is recognized as those with, little power, keeping His word, and they have not denied His name. Because the members of the church of Laodicea are lukewarm, Jesus said He will spit them out of His mouth because of their pride in three ways, they say, 1) I am rich, 2) I have prospered and 3) I need nothing. This makes six churches each being recognized with three traits. Only one is recognized in a positive way (Revelation 2 & 3)

John described God's throne as three precious stones (Revelation 4).

The creatures sang "Holy, holy, holy" three times and identified He who sits on the throne in three ways: **the one who was, who is, and who will come in perfection** (Revelation 4).

The seven eyes of the Lord are mentioned three times in the Bible (Zechariah 3:9, 4:10, and Revelation 5:6).

Five times in Revelation, three words are used to describe the worthiness of the Lamb, His glory, His honor and His power. There are other words used also which we will get into later (Revelation 4, 5, 7, 19).

When the first seal is broken in the latter days, the angel will deliver three judgments of hail, fire, and blood on the earth (Revelation 8).

Three woes are given to the next three angels about to blow their trumpets (Revelation 8).

An army appears for destruction wearing three colors: a red-orange, black, and yellow at the first woe (Revelation 9). The second woe will be a great earthquake (Revelation 11). The third woe will be a prism of colors, lightning, and thunder coming from the Ark of the Covenant from inside the Temple (Revelation 11).

The beast is described three times in Revelation as having seven heads, ten horns with seven crowns (Revelation 12,13,&17).

The beast is described as cunning as a leopard, as powerful as a bear, and with a mouth like a devouring lion (Revelation 13).

The dragon gives the beast his power, his seat, and great authority (Revelation 13).

Saints in the last days are to endure, keep His Commandments, and keep faith in Jesus. The Son of man reaps the harvest using three angels (Revelation 14).

Three demonic frogs come out of the mouths of the dragon, the beast, and the false prophet (Revelation 16).

Jerusalem will be split into three parts and have large hailstones fall on them (Revelation 16).

Three counterfeit qualities of the beast: he was, he is not, and is to come only to descend to the bottomless pit (Revelation 17).

War will be made against those with the Lamb, but the Lamb of God wins. Those with Him are 1) called, 2) faithful, and 3) are true (Revelation 17).

The world stands back and watches Babylon as she burns. Three times, it is mentioned that Babylon will be destroyed in an hour (Revelation 18).

There are three physical descriptions of the seven spirits of God in front of the throne of God. The first being seven lamp stands, the second as a lamb with seven horns, and the third as a lamb having seven eyes (Revelation 4 & 5). This symbolizes that three (the trinity) plus seven (spirits) equals ten, or "perfect complete holiness" (Revelation 19). More on this later.

Heaven is opened up and behold a white horse. He who is on the white horse is 1) faithful, 2) true and 3) with righteousness, His purpose is to make war. His white robe is dipped in blood and He has three names: the "Word of God" being the first. From his mouth issues a two edged sword to judge the world. His other two names are inscribed on his thigh. The other two names are King of kings, and Lord of lords (Revelation 19). These two names bear witness to the "Word."

There are three imitations of God with the beast: Satan, the beast, and the false prophet (Revelation 20).

The antichrist, 1) was, 2) is not, and 3) will descend to the bottomless pit (Revelation 20); this is the second time this is mentioned, the first being in Revelation 17. This is to bear witness or to confirm God's word about the antichrist.

Last Days Review

A new heaven and earth is described. Along with a New Jerusalem and a new temple where God will dwell with men. Eternal life will mean 1) no death, 2) no tears and 3) no more pain. The set of three gates that face four directions have three angels at each gate. There are also twelve foundations to the wall. The city is described in three ways: 1) with walls of Jasper, 2) as a city of gold and 3) being transparent. The foundations are adorned with twelve types of precious stones with three new names of each of the disciples at each gate. The twelve gates are like twelve pearls. Three things will remain eternal, 1) there will be no need for light, for He will be the light, 2) The glory of the Lord will fill the city, and 3) there will be no evil, only His righteousness (Revelation 21).

It is important to recognize that Jesus at the end of Revelations states, all the information that has been given to John was also to be given to the churches. This proves that the message to the churches was not just for that time but symbolic and relevant to the last day churches. That is, the events in the latter days that have just been written about by John. Jesus again identifies himself with an additional three factors of recognition; He is the root, the offspring of David, and the bright morning star. This is the seventh time Jesus identified Himself in three ways to the churches. The request for Jesus to come is mentioned three times: the spirit and the bride say, "come," he who hears, says, "come," and he who is thirsty says, "come." Jesus states three times He will come quickly; again, three sets of three. Also in the last chapter of the Bible, we are given three truths, three promises and three invitations, a making of a formula for a "perfect ending" (Revelation 22).

In this last chapter of the Bible, Jesus reveals His authority, His qualifications if you will, in three ways. There are three requests for His return. He claims three times to return which is interpreted as a" perfect promise." These three sets each contain three points. If we put this in a number format, it would be 333, a number that represents a "perfect God with a perfect plan and a perfect ending." Compare that to the counterfeit of the antichrist, 666 (Revelation 22). I know this is repeated, but it is meant to drive home the importance of understanding this.

The Jews today still celebrate a time of three weeks of fasting called Shiva Asar B 'Tammus. This is a time of recognizing the devastating destruction of the temple twice. Once by the Romans and once by King Nebuchadnezzar. Upon the return of Jesus, the Lord himself at the end of the tribulation will build the third and perfect temple (Zachariah 6 KJV).

NOTES

Section Four

The Number Four

Four represents judgment or gives warning. It is a number that is primarily used within the books of prophecy pertaining to the last days. It can also represent a sum of two numbers such as three plus one equals four (3+1=4). This would be interpreted as a "perfect God qualified to pronounce judgment."

Four judgments or disasters came upon Job, and four will come upon the world. In Jeremiah, we learn four judgments will come upon Jerusalem. Ezekiel described four creatures each with four faces and four wings. Each creature is in charge of four wheels within wheels until the designated time of judgment upon the earth. These wheels symbolize time rolling or going forward.

Daniel received a vision of what will happen in the last days. Through history, there will be four kingdoms on earth representing Babylon, the last one during the last days. Daniel described a man from a vision with seven descriptions; a head, chest, belly, thighs, legs, feet, and ten toes (the toes could represent the ten kings in Revelation). He described a stone uncut by human hands that destroys the feet.

Four things have been given to this king: the kingdom, the power, the might, and the glory. The fourth kingdom to rise will be strong as iron mixed with clay. It shall be a divided kingdom (politically, religiously, and or by race). This divided kingdom will come together with a common cause, but they are still separate, as iron and clay do not mix together. They will be destroyed by God's kingdom (Daniel 2).

Babylon is both literal and symbolic at the same time representing three things: a culture, a time, and a female spirit named Babylon, which means "man's self-indulgence and the imperfection of man." The three definitions of the prophetic Babylon, represent the sum of the three definitions that makes the whole. It is a culture, it is an actual spirit named Babylon, and it refers to a time and place in the world. It can be separated or combined, depending on the context.

In Daniel, we learn the last kingdom, recognized as the fourth kingdom of Babylon will be the one of judgment. The kingdom's ruler will be very powerful and secretly devour the earth; his purpose will be fulfilled by lies and deception. It will be a time of Babylon, or when men wallow in self-indulgence. This leader will be a descendant from the Middle East, primarily from ancient Persia and more specifically the area of the Medes, which is now Iran. He will be out to destroy the descendants of Greece.

Then we are told the end will come from the four corners of the earth just before the trumpet is blown, and God's wrath is released on earth. In the description of the new temple, there are four tables outside the temple to be used for a sin offering. This is an interesting passage for it is in reference to the new temple in the New Jerusalem when Jesus returns.

God's wrath is set in stone, so to speak. In Amos, we learn that even for the sake of four righteous men, God will not change His mind about the judgment and wrath to come upon man. We are told in Zechariah that four horsemen are going back and forth between heaven and earth, waiting for the final judgment.

Remember when the soldiers tore Christ's robe when He was hanging on the cross? It is strange that this small tidbit of information was recorded, but it was torn into four pieces. Consider this; that perhaps somehow, this act depicted Jesus as the one of judgment to come; it could also mean that those who tore His garment will stand in judgment.

Here is a convicting and clarifying use of number four often overlooked. Revelation 1–3 refers to the seven churches. The seven churches did historically exist, however the message is to those who are in the church or claiming to follow Christ in the end times. The seven churches represent those people in the latter days who will claim to follow Jesus. Each follower of Christ will fall into one of the categories of religious worship noted in the seven churches; God calls four churches to repent or be thrown in with unbelievers. This should be understood that not all that proclaim to be Christians are necessarily saved. In Matthew 7, the Lord explains that not every one that calls on his name or heals the sick or cast out demons will enter into the kingdom of heaven. He goes on to say, "Depart from me, for I never knew you." This one passage alone reveals the teaching of eternal salvation should be questioned. This is confirmed in the last two chapters of Revelation, when John is told to give the message (Revelation) to the churches. In the end, the day of the Lord, death will come on humanity in four ways: pestilence, war, famine, and destruction (natural disasters that include fire).

Number Four References

The punishment for sin extends to the third and fourth generations (Exodus 20, 34). The Lord called Samuel three times, but Samuel did not recognize His voice. Samuel answered the fourth time the Lord called his name and learned the Lord was going to punish (judge) the house of his father, Eli, for disobedience (1 Samuel 3).

Four disasters happened to Job (Job 1).

Four judgments of destruction come upon the world: desolation, destruction, famine, and war (Isaiah 51).

Four kinds of destroyers for judgment are sent upon Jerusalem (Jeremiah 15).

Ezekiel saw four men-like creatures coming from the north, each with four heads with four different faces and four wings. They had human hands and faces of men in front, lions on the right, oxen on the left, and eagles in the back. In the midst of them was something like torches, fire and lightning. They were waiting for the time of destruction. The four wheels of time are described as wheels within wheels (Ezekiel 1, 10; Revelation).

The end will come from the four corners of the earth. God's wrath will be poured out, and the trumpet is blown (Ezekiel 7, Revelation).

Ezekiel sees four abominations of Israel (Ezekiel 8).

Four judgments will afflict Israel: war, beasts, famine, and pestilence (Ezekiel 13, 14).

The Lord shall send four sore acts of judgment on the world: the sword, famine, evil beasts, and pestilence (Ezekiel 14 & 15).

The Lord rebuked the people four times because they did not obey Him and they polluted the Sabbath (Ezekiel 20).

There are four tables in the temple and outside the new temple for sin offerings (Ezekiel 40–43).

The last Babylon is split into four pieces by a large earthquake (Jeremiah 50–52).

King Nebuchadnezzar had a dream in which Daniel not only describes the actual meaning but also gives the meaning of the dream. Daniel clarified to Nebuchadnezzar that his God was in charge of all who rule and those who do not rule kingdoms. It was a vision of what is to happen in the last days—four kingdoms (periods) of Babylon, the last being one of judgment. Daniel describes an image of a man with seven physical descriptions. Then a stone (rock of salvation) that is uncut by human hands destroys the feet. Four things have been given to the last king: the kingdom, the power, the might, and the glory. The fourth kingdom to rise will be strong as iron but mixed with clay. It shall be a divided kingdom, most likely politically and religiously. This kingdom is destroyed by Gods kingdom. Babylon is not only symbolic of a life style accepted by man. It is also a name of a spirit that controls certain people, at certain time periods that God has allowed to complete his plan of redemption and His plan of judgment for all of mankind. When Daniel was given this information, he was in the third time period or what is referred to as the Babylonian empire. It ruled most of the earth at that time. It was an empire that stood for mans rights and justice for all people. Does this sound familiar? (Daniel 2)

Four men are observed in the fire when only three had been thrown into it for refusing to worship the king as God (Daniel 3). This is an another example of four achieved by a sum of two numbers, three plus one in this case, symbolizing the "perfect deliverer from judgment" to those of faith. Remember that God is our deliverer, He is number one.

Four kingdoms (periods of time, cultures) are referred to as Babylon. The last kingdom will be at the end of the world, when God's wrath comes upon the earth (Daniel 2 & 7).

In Daniel, a second vision is received again referring to the last days, this confirms the first. Four winds were stirred up against the sea. Four beasts sent for destruction came out of the sea. The first was like a lion with wings of an eagle. The wings were plucked off, and the creature stood like a man. The second, a bear, rose with three ribs in its mouth and was told to eat much flesh. The third was like a leopard with four wings like a bird and having four heads, and it was given dominion. The fourth beast represents the fourth kingdom of Babylon, which will devour the earth. The fourth beast is very powerful and had ten horns, defined as ten kings (Daniel 7; compare with Revelation).

The fourth and last kingdom of Persia (Babylon) is rich and prosperous. The king will stir up his people against the descendants of Greece. He will be a mighty king and do what he wants. When he has risen to the top of his kingdom, his kingdom will be broken into four parts and divided toward the four winds of heaven, and his kingdom will be removed from him and given to four others (Daniel 10–11). This division will be created by a huge earthquake that will split the nation into four parts.

The four kings spoken of reflect periods of time that allow us to recognize the proximity of the end. The fourth being the last and the era of judgment (Daniel 11).

Even for four righteous men, God will not turn away from His wrath upon man. He is set on achieving His punishment to the nations (Amos 1–4).

Four horns or four leaders that are skilled in destruction come against the leader of the Gentiles who goes against Israel and scatters it (Zechariah 1).

Four horsemen go back and forth between heaven and earth, waiting to bring judgment (Zechariah 1–2).

He will spread His people as the four winds from heaven (Zechariah 1–2).

Four chariots with four angels will appear between two mountains of brass at the end, upon the return of Jesus. This is at the end of the tribulation (Zechariah 6, Revelation).

Four angels and four winds will come from the four corners of the earth to destroy (Zechariah 6).

Four requirements for the saints in the end times, speak the truth, seek peace, have clean hearts, and make no false oaths (Zechariah 8).

Joseph was told in four dreams to go to Egypt, Israel, Galilee, and Nazareth (Matthew 1–2).

The garment of Jesus when crucified is torn into four pieces by the soldiers (John 18–19).

God offers us wisdom, righteousness, sanctification, and redemption, four spiritual precepts, through Jesus (1 Corinthians 1).

In the first three chapters of Revelation, God called out to the church, the professing believers, to repent four times. He acknowledges four good things about the church at Ephesus: they have endured, they have been patient, their labor, and they have not grown weary. But they have strayed from their first love and He calls for their repentance or else He will remove the candlestick from them. The candlestick refers to the spirit of God. To him who conquers the tree of life is given (Revelation 2). What happens to the person in the church who has faith, but does not conquer or loses his faith?

Around the throne of God are four creatures with eyes all around them (Revelation 4).

In the fourth seal, the rider of the horse is Death, and Hades followed him. They are given power to kill one fourth of humanity in four ways: sword, famine, pestilence, and wild beasts (Revelation 6).

Four angels at the four corners of the earth will hold back the winds and wait for the day and hour of judgment. Another angel appears from the "rising of the sun" and he calls out to the angels to hold back from destroying the earth until all of the servants of God are sealed upon their forehead. That number is twelve thousand out of each of the twelve tribes of Israel (Revelation 7). Note the antichrist also seals his followers on the forehead that is represented by the number 666.

Another angel mixed prayers with incense from a golden censer and threw it to the earth, which caused thunder, voices, lightning, and an earthquake (Revelation 8).

When the fourth angel blows his horn, four things will happen: 1) a third of the sun was struck, 2) a third of the moon and 3) a third of the stars, 4) a third of the day and night was kept from shinning (Revelation 8). Note that you have a total of four thirds or "judgment over perfection."

When the sixth trumpet is blown, four angels waiting for the hour, the day, the month, and the year to kill one third of mankind (*twice ten thousand times ten thousand*) of the troops (Revelation 9). At this point, a little less than half of mankind will exist (Revelation 6, 9).

A voice proclaimed that 1) salvation, 2) strength, 3) the kingdom of God, and 4) the power of Christ has come (Revelation 12).

The seventh angel poured his bowl into the air, and a voice came from the throne, saying, "It is finished." Four events happen, lightning, voices, thunder, and a huge earthquake occur, destroying everything (Revelation 16; compare this with Revelation 8).

John hears another voice of a command from the Lord to take His people out of Babylon so they would not have to partake in the punishment of Babylon's sin. Four things happen in one hour: death, mourning, famine, and burning with fire (Revelation 18).

One of the seven angels comes to John and shows him the New Jerusalem with a great wall around it. There are three gates each facing four directions for a total of twelve gates. Each gate has three angels guarding the gates, for a total of thirty six angels (Revelation 21).

Four judgments will come against, the evil doers, the filthy, the righteous, and the holy (Revelation 22); these are two judgments for the unrighteous and two for the righteous. This cannot be changed; it is "confirmed judgment", this is understood by identifying the sum of two plus two equals four. Please note that in this passage everyone is judged, the righteous and the unrighteous.

Interesting Notes on Four

The seven spirits of God are mentioned in Revelation four times.

There are four sets of seven in the book of Revelation, the book of judgment: seven churches, seven seals, seven trumpets, and seven bowls of wrath pertaining to judgment. The message hidden within the message is this; seven means completion, four is judgment; put together, it is the "completion of judgment, or judgment made complete."

Within the context of the seven churches are seven promises. The terminology used pertaining to the believers to conquer or overcome (KJV) the world is used five times. You will discover that five means "a sign for man". I believe this is meant to be interpreted as their faith is meant to be a sign to the rest of the world. Four churches are called to repent, while the other three churches are called to be 1) faithful, 2) watchful, 3) to remember, 4) to keep His word and 5) to hold fast. The third one mentioned above "to remember" refers to acknowledging what God has done and who He is. Three is perfection, four is judgment, and five is a sign (Revelation 1–3). In context, seven churches, seven promises; four churches called to repent, three are called to remain faithful in five ways as a sign. Four churches are each given three descriptions of the person or character of Christ. This is full of symbols within the numbers, stay with me. Here is where we begin to see the breakdown and symbolism of numbers within numbers. Those who claim to follow Christ and want to be made complete in Christ will be judged. Only three out of seven followers of Jesus will be considered righteous and perfect and will be signs for everyone else. The other four will be thrown in with the hypocrites and unbelievers. In Revelation 1 and in Revelation 22; we are told that the message of the book is aimed at the churches in the last days. In other words, these seven churches represent seven categories in which all believers will be classified or will be identified with regarding their faith in the end times.

Here is a very important insight found in Revelation 3 where the believers in Sardis are being addressed. In the King James Version, Jesus challenges them to be watchful and to remember what they have received and heard, to hold fast and to repent. If they do not watch, they will not know the hour that He will come upon them. However, there are a few within the church that will receive white robes and their names will not be blotted out of the book of life. This passage indicates that true believers will somehow know the hour because they are watching for His return.

To the church of Philadelphia, the Lord states that due to their obedience and patience he will keep them from the hour of temptation, which will come upon the world. The word temptation here in the original Greek is "testing." The believers are told to hold fast so that their crown will not be removed. He is saying to stand firm in our faith, so we are not deceived, in order that we be delivered from his wrath. This indicates an apparent rapture of the saints. What happens to those that do not stand firm and are deceived? Scriptures teach that in that day some will lose their faith. By the way, Babylon is destroyed somewhere in the middle of the seven year tribulation.

Then we see in Revelation chapter 18, Babylon is destroyed and becomes a dwelling place for demons and evil spirits. John hears a command from heaven for the over comers to come out of her, so they do not have to receive what is about to fall upon Babylon. Babylon is then destroyed in one hour. It is stated that Babylon is a city, the word city in this passage, in the original Greek literally means an area surrounded by walls or is somehow protected, perhaps in this case, by military power, water or God. It is possible that the nation was once a nation "under God". Later God removing his hedge or wall from that nation due to their iniquities. It is also common to name a city, and in doing so, it represents a country or a nation. If we were to say Jerusalem, it represents Israel. If we say Paris, it represents France. If we say Washington D.C., it represents the United States. The point here is just before the destruction of Babylon, it appears that at least some of the believers that have been tested and overcome, are saved from God's wrath. We are told that in that hour there will be plagues, mourning, famine and fire. Only four small parts will remain of Babylon after a great earthquake (Jeremiah 50-52 KJV).

The last four words in Revelation spoken by Jesus are, "I will come quickly" (Revelation 22). What happens upon His return but judgment?

Section Five

The Number Five

Five represents a sign to help see, to prove, or to demonstrate God to man.
Genesis 45 contains another reference to numbers in numbers. Joseph revealed to his brothers who he was in the second year of a famine. He said there would be an additional five years of famine, but they were not to worry; the Lord would provide. First, note that his revealing came at the end of two years with five to go. If you use the previous information, this would be interpreted as two plus five equals seven, "a confirmed sign that would result in completion". This event brings Jacob (Israel) to Egypt, the beginning of the nation Israel under the authority of Egypt, just as God had planned. This situation fell into the "complete plan of God". Then, some four hundred years later, God frees the Israelites through Moses.

When Moses was called by the Lord to lead the Israelites out of Egypt, Moses kept coming up with excuses, five of them. The last excuse was that he had a speech problem. So the Lord allowed Aaron to be Moses' spokesman. The two led Israel out of Egypt, and both witnessed the works of God with the Israelites. I'm not sure if this is anything, but it is interesting that there were five excuses and two men. Could it be that five answers to Moses from the Lord was a sign to him confirmed?

Remember when Jesus fed five thousand men plus women and children with five loaves of bread and two fish, and had twelve baskets of food left over? If you were to decode this and recognize the significance in the numbers, it could be understood in this way: five plus two equals seven with a remainder of twelve, "a sign with confirmation completed with authority." Why was this important enough to be recorded in the Word? Why did Jesus specifically have twelve left over? This sign was referring to Jesus, and the event was meant to be a sign to mankind confirming who Jesus was. Doesn't this seem strange? It doesn't add up mathematically, but it is meant to be a message, a perfect example of God's message in numbers.

Twelve, we will learn, represents "authority." Many times in Scriptures, seven consists of a breakdown of five plus two or a combination of two other numbers. Seven represents "completion," more on this when we get to seven and twelve. Can you start seeing a pattern here of numbers building off other numbers? Each number represents a hidden mystery of God and His works. You will also see the significance of the five thousand men.

In the covering of the Ark of the Covenant, the Lord specified eleven curtains over the top or on the outside of the roof of the tent or tabernacle. Five were to go on one side, over the top, and six on the other side, over the top. This is an example of the representation of numbers in numbers. This was a sign (five) and a reminder to man (six) of God's covering over them and the ark of the covenant every time they looked up to the tabernacle (Exodus 26, 36).

David slew the giant with one of five stones he picked out of a stream. Only one was needed to kill Goliath, but the five stones were meant as a sign to Israel. Goliath had mocked Israel for forty days; the Israelites were in fear of their lives due to the Philistines who wanted to draw them into war with them. The five stones were symbolic as a "sign" to Israel. God represented the "one" stone, the defender of Israel, their rock of salvation. This was a story of a child having faith and a reminder to all Israelites that the one and only God was with them. The one stone within the five stones was a sign to Israel that the Lord would provide, that He is able to be their defender.

In the last days, locust-like creatures will sting those who have taken the mark of the beast for five months; those that have not taken the mark on their foreheads will escape this torment and be protected for the five months from these scorpion like creatures. Those who follow God will be a sign, (number five), to those who do not follow God and the consequences for receiving the mark of the beast. This indicates that the saints are still here for at least part of the seven year tribulation.

Number Five References

The famine during the time of Joseph was described as two plus five years (Genesis 45). It was described earlier when Joseph was a lad in a dream, as seven years.
Benjamin's booty was five times more than his brothers' booty (Genesis 42–43).
Moses gave God five excuses why he was not the man to lead Israel out of Egypt. Each time the Lord answered him. Upon the fifth time, Moses finally agreed to obey God. God gave a "sign" of His calling to Moses, a burning bush that was not consumed and the voice of God came from it (Exodus 3, 4).
Noah's ark, the ark of the covenant, the original temple, and the new temple have many references to derivatives of five, the most common being fifty or five times ten. We will get into this later.

David picked out five stones to kill Goliath (1 Samuel 17). Only one was needed and only one was used.

David requested five loaves of bread when escaping from King Saul (1 Samuel 21–22).

Five angels will be sent to destroy Israel in the end (Ezekiel 9).

Joseph had five dreams about Jesus, the first from an angel telling him of Mary's pregnancy and four more to tell him to move to different places (Matthew 1–2). Is this perhaps a "sign" that Jesus was the Chosen One for judgment (four plus one equals five)?

Jesus fed five thousand men plus women and children with five loaves of bread and two fish and had twelve baskets of food left over (Matthew 14).

To the church of Ephesus: This is from him who holds the seven stars and walks among the seven lamp stands. He knows of their 1) works, 2) their toil, 3) their patient endurance, 4) how they hate evil and have tested their teachers and found many of them to be false and 5) that they hate the deeds of the Nicolaitans. Here, five positive qualities of the church were recognized yet they are told to repent (Revelation 2).It is obvious that they are exposed as going through the motions, judged for not having a true relationship with God.

To the church of Laodicea. Because the church is lukewarm, (KJV) He will spit them out of His mouth because of their pride in three ways, they say, I am rich, I have prospered and I need nothing. They fail to recognize that they are 1) wretched, 2) miserable, 3) poor, 4) blind and 5) naked. Note here we have five negative things about the church pointed out (Revelation 3). Five negative responses are given to them and they too are told to repent. Could the church or believers in Ephesus and those identified with those in Laodicea be "confirmed signs" to the believers to be right with God or be judged by God?

In the latter days, those without the mark of God on their foreheads will be tormented for five months by the sting of locust-like creatures (Revelation 9).

In the end, God's temple will be opened and the ark of the covenant will be seen inside; from it will come, 1) lightning, 2) thunder, 3) voices, 4) an earthquake and 5) hail. This is a "sign" to all of creation and all humanity revealing the power and authority of God (Revelation 11).

NOTES

Section Six

The Number Six

Six represents mankind, freedom, the pride of man, incomplete, imperfect.
We first see six appear in Genesis; man was created on the sixth day; this symbolizes that six is man's number. It also represents the freedom that mankind can do what they want, the freedom even for self-indulgence, or self-centeredness away from God. This freedom results in the "pride of man," pride in what he is able to accomplish.

We also see in scripture that God designated man to work six days and rest on the seventh. This was by God's design so we would focus on Him, not ourselves, and not get caught up in the pride of life but take time to worship God.

We are told both in Revelation and in Isaiah, there are four angels each with six wings that sing praise to God continuously.

In Jeremiah and in Ezekiel, we see that to the Jews, six represented liberty and freedom. Slaves were to be set free after six years. When Israel and Judah failed to obey this law established by God, they received His wrath; thousands were killed. This may appear on the outside to be a rather harsh judgment, but I believe God wanted to establish the important symbolism behind six; He wanted to reveal the pride mankind takes in freedom from God. This established the importance of the number six, especially the number 666, when God's wrath will again come on all mankind. We must understand the symbolism of numbers to understand what God's hidden message is. Remember that three represents perfection, whether it is the number three or another number repeated three times. This is referred to as a "set" of numbers. Six is important to God; if we understand that three represents perfection, and that six repeated three times should be recognized as a set of three numbers, described as 666, or "pursuing man's perfect system of taking care of everyone and establishing liberty and rights for all."

Remember that Jesus was on the cross for six hours; it was defined as a set of two three hour periods. Again symbolizing his "perfect death for man", by the use of number three and six. In the last days, we see the perfect counterfeit with a set of three numbers, 666, representing the antichrist. This is no accident!

In the last days, when God's wrath will destroy the world, there will be a government or culture referred to as Babylon. This will be in the fourth period of time or kingdom referred to in Daniel. This will be the last kingdom on the earth, the final (fourth) judgment. At that time, this country will be compared to Sodom and Gomorrah, which were two cities that God sent fire upon from heaven and destroyed them. Scriptures teach that history repeats itself; the last kingdom will be guilty of the same sins as Sodom.

Interestingly enough, there are six of them, defined or symbolizing "mans sin." This is the guilt of Sodom, the same guilt of which the last Babylon will be full of. They will be full of 1) pride, 2) in need of nothing, 3) enjoying the abundance of idleness, 4) indifferent to the poor and needy, 5) they are haughty, and 6) they accept sexual abominations and the promotion of homosexuality. This Babylon or culture at that time will also promote freedom and rights for everyone, rich or poor. Equality for all will be sought, but not found.

The number 666 represents the perfect promotion of freedom and peace for mankind or the ultimate time of man; it makes everyone equal and cared for on a global basis. The number 666 represents the "perfect system of man, for man, by man". It must be noted that the antichrist (the beast) will cause everyone to receive the mark on the forehead or the right hand in order to buy or sell anything. This calls for wisdom; "let him who has understanding recognize the number of the beast, for it is a human number, number six hundred and sixty six" (Revelation 18). If one worships this man (the beast) and his image and receives the mark on the forehead or on his hand, they also shall drink the wine of God's wrath. This is poured unmixed into the cup of the Lord's anger. They will be tormented with fire and sulfur in the presence of the holy angels and in the presence of the Lamb for eternity. They shall have no rest day or night; these will be those that receive the mark of the beast. "Here is a call for the endurance of the saints, those who keep the commandments of God and the faith in Jesus" (Revelation14). Note this last verse indicates the saints are still here.

I think it is interesting to point out here something overlooked about the period referred to as "that day" in Isaiah 31 and 32. It has been mistranslated in some of the newer Bible translations. In the original King James Version, Isaiah refers to the era of the antichrist. His reference could be regarding the false prophet that comes prior to the anti-Christ, or the anti-Christ, it is not clear. A time in which a ruler of a particular nation (a king) will be recognized as a "vile" man. In Hebrew, the word "vile" refers to being wicked, disgraceful and dishonorable. He will be a master of liars and will perform whirlwinds of confusion. The Koran refers to this man as one who causes a time of chaos. His purpose is to secretly destroy the middle class and seemingly eliminate people being poor, a redistribution of wealth if you will. His true intensions are to have two classes of people, the poor and the rich. "He will be a liberal and his plans of deception will be by liberal ways, and he will pursue liberal things, and by liberal things shall he stand." He will talk prosperity, but his purpose is to deceive. The original word "liberal" in the Hebrew literally means noble, to offer himself as a soldier, perhaps an enemy soldier to the God of the Jews. This man will be about reform, rights, and the promotion of people protected by civil liberties.

One other time the term "liberal" is used in the Old Testament in Proverbs 11, again in the original King James Version. In this context, it refers to one who speaks of prosperity. This is a case where two words are interchangeable. For the sake of demonstration only, I will use the words "liberal and democrat" as two words that are somewhat interchangeable. In Proverbs, the original Hebrew for the word "liberal" is written as "Berakah" and pronounced as "baw-rak" which implies prosperity. It is a derivative of a word from another ancient Hebrew word, "Barak" which means to curse God, blaspheme, to claim to be a benefit to God. This is where I would like to quote out of Revelation 2, "He who has an ear, let him hear what the Spirit says to the churches." Like I said, I just thought this was interesting, nothing more, well until my next book. Some may take this as being politically incorrect- I am just quoting the Bible. I am sure there are those that will want this documented. Look up the word "liberal" in the Abingdon's Strong's exhaustive Concordance of the Bible, forty- first printing, 1981.

Number Six References

Man was created on the sixth day (Genesis 2).

Abraham bargained with the Lord six times to save Sodom and Gomorrah (Genesis 18).

The Israelites were to gather manna for only six days a week (Exodus 16).

Six days are designated for work (Exodus 20).

God called Moses and seventy elders to climb part way up Mt. Sinai prior to giving him the Ten Commandments. Moses sacrificed some animals and decreed that the blood was a confirmation of the covenant the Lord had made with them. Before Moses went up the mountain, the Lord's glory rested on the mountaintop for six days. On the seventh day, Moses was called to the top, where he remained for forty days and received the laws of God (Exodus 24).

Sixty-six days were required for purification of a woman who gave birth to a female (Leviticus 12).

Six cities were designated as places of refuge for those accused of murder (Numbers 35).

There were Giants with six fingers on each hand and six toes on each foot revealed (2 Samuel 21).

Solomon received 666 talents of gold in one year (1 Kings 10).

Isaiah saw angels with six wings worshipping the Lord (Isaiah 6).

When Judah was attacked by Babylon around 500 BC, Zedekiah decreed that slaves were to be released every six years. They refused to continue this decree, originally established by God. Consequently, they suffered from war, famine, and disease and were scattered around the world. This penalty for disobedience will be repeated in the last days (Jeremiah 34).

The guilt of Sodom was due to 1) pride, 2) not in need of anything, 3) abundance of idleness, 4) did not help the poor and needy, 5) haughty, and 6) abominable sexual behavior (Ezekiel 16).

Six angels in human form will appear at the north gate at the beginning of the end of Israel in the latter days to destroy those in Jerusalem without the mark of God on their foreheads. God shows no pity. They start with the seventy elders and kill them in the temple. The rest of the dead are thrown into the temple to defile it (Ezekiel 9). It is also interesting to note the counterfeit, the anti-christ; he too marks the foreheads of his followers in the Book of Revelations.

King Belshazzar of Babylon worshipped six things made by man (Daniel 5).

Jesus was on the cross for six hours, symbolizing His death for man (Mark 15).

Elizabeth was six months pregnant with John when Mary informed her, that she too would conceive a son and his name would be Jesus (Luke 1).

We are told not to entertain six earthly emotions: bitterness, wrath, anger, clamor, slander, and malice (Ephesians 4).

Members of the church of Thyatira were known for six virtues: their works, love, faith, service, patience, and their works to be more than the first. However, God has this against them, that they tolerate Jezebel (a spirit of pollution, of self-centeredness) who is teaching his servants to practice sin (Revelation 2).

Four angels with six wings each worship the Lord continuously. Their wings are covered with eyes (Revelation 4).

On delivery of the sixth seal in the latter days, six disasters will occur: a great earthquake, the sun turning black, the moon becoming like blood, stars falling from heaven, heaven departing like a scroll with all the mountains and islands moving, and all mankind trying to hide from God's wrath (Revelation 6).

In the last years, the mark of the beast will be 666. **Here is a call for the endurance of the saints in their faith.** Another beast with two horns appearing to be like a lamb and speaking like a dragon will appear. He will force everyone to worship the beast or be killed and will perform miracles. He will make an image of the beast that will breathe and talk. He will cause everyone to be marked on the right hand or forehead to buy or sell anything. The number is of man, 666. Whoever receives the mark of the beast shall receive the fullness of God's wrath and eternal damnation (Revelation 13 and 14). Notice the set of three repeated numbers of number six: it is to be interpreted as the "perfect system of man, or the perfect incomplete, self centered man, the ultimate time of man." The mark is possibly a computer chip somehow meshed with man's DNA to avoid theft and for positive ID. It will be used on a global basis. It will be easy and accurate, and it will make sense and will eliminate the need for cash and credit cards. It will eliminate fraud. Everything will be purchased by the mark, including food and all medical care.

Six kinds of sinners will be outside New Jerusalem: dogs, sorcerers, fornicators, murderers, idolaters, and those who do not hold to the truth, or liars (Revelation 22). The dogs referred to here are the people that are devouring; they are lacking any moral character. The Hebrew word used for dogs in many cases referred to male prostitutes. They return to their vomit (sinful life style) and are sexually indiscreet and considered to be a low life, full of greed and self indulgence (Exodus 11, Proverbs 26, Isaiah 56, Philippians 3).

NOTES

Section Seven

The Number Seven

Seven can represent a time of rest, cleansing, purification, or completion, depending on its context. Right from the beginning in Genesis, we are told that the creation process took seven days, or periods. It took these symbolic seven days to "complete" all creation. Then on the seventh day, God rested.

Here He set an example for mankind and later designated to man to rest on the seventh day as a law. From the beginning, the concepts of "completion and rest" were affiliated with seven.

A few chapters later, we learn God was fed up with man and decided to cleanse the world by destroying it with a great flood. Noah and his family were the only ones selected to survive the cleansing or purification process. God established with Noah the significance and importance of numbers. He was directed to take two of every kind of animal on the ark and seven pair of each clean animal. Gathering all the animals took seven days.

Once the animals were aboard, God closed the doors, and Noah was in the ark for seven days before it began to rain. Then it rained for forty days and forty nights until the earth was cleansed or washed clean, if you will. The water was fifteen cubits higher than the tallest mountain. When the rain stopped, the ark floated for 150 days before coming to rest on a mountain in the seventh month. Noah sent a bird to check for dry land three times, each seven days apart. The third time, the bird did not return to the ark, indicating there was dry land once again. Did you note all the sevens in these events? Can you see the significance of the amount and the timing of the birds?

Remember that three represents "perfection;" seven means "completion and purification." With respect to this cleansing of the world, we can see a formula within the story, three plus seven which is interpreted as "perfect and complete purification". Here is another insight of the numbers to come. Ten represents holiness; if we add three and seven, we get ten. The releasing of the birds symbolizes the flood was the sum of the whole. Translated it would mean the "perfect and complete purging of the earth that equals holiness." How does holiness relate to the flood? If we reverse the formula we see that God simply through His wrath made the earth "holy in a complete and perfect way" (ten equals seven plus three).

47

Three and seven are continuously repeated in the last seven years of wrath in Revelation. Again, the use of numbers depicts God's "perfect and complete holiness to come." The world was purified once during Noah's time and will be purified again the second time "confirmed," in the seven years of tribulation, which is coming very soon; we are at the doorstep of it as this is written. Perhaps the door is already opened and we are now standing at the threshold.

It should start being noticed that there are several ways to break down numbers within numbers and that each formula depicts something different about the event in which it is used. For instance, the number seven can be a sum of three plus four, two plus five, or six plus one. The interpretation depends upon the numbers used within the context. In some cases, you can have the translation of the numbers to have several meanings, which somehow still work.

If we broke down "seven" using the three formulas mentioned above and put them in the context of Noah and the flood, there would be three messages within the number seven. Three plus four would be "the perfect judgment of God that equals purification." Two plus five would be a "confirmed sign to man that equals perfect cleansing." Six plus one within this context would mean, "Man without God, equals perfect judgment (three plus four)." Using these same breakdowns or formulas, they can also be applied to God's judgment in Revelation, a message within the message.

The prophets gave warnings from God that revealed His secrets of the judgment to come using numbers. Many times, seven is designated as "two plus five" in prophecy or two sets of three and a half years. More of this is explained in the section Numbers within Numbers. Seven is used in prophecy in the New and the Old Testaments. This repeated warning over thousands of years by different people, reveals the numbers two plus five, as a "confirmed sign, that equals completion and or cleansing," leaving no question to His plan.

When Israel was in Egypt and Moses was asking for the release of God's people, it was the last event that got Pharaoh's attention. Moses told the people not to eat leavened bread for seven days. On the seventh day, the angel of death killed the firstborn males of Egypt but passed over those who had put blood over their door mantels and had eaten unleavened bread for seven days. This was the beginning of Passover for the Jewish nation. A celebration that lasts for seven days, even today.

When the people came to Mount Sinai, a cloud hung around it, and the glory of the Lord was in the cloud. On the seventh day, God told Moses to ascend the mountain and receive the laws of God.

Later, when Moses was completing the Tent of Meeting, the Lord designated to have seven lamp stands to hold seven torches in front of the Ark of the Covenant. According to Revelation these are the seven spirits of God named by Isaiah: They are 1) The Spirit of the Lord, 2) The Spirit of wisdom, 3) The Spirit of understanding, 4) The Spirit of counsel, 5) The Spirit of might, 6) The Spirit of knowledge, and 7) The Spirit of the fear of the Lord. These seven spirits coexist with the trinity, and are to be recognized as seven additional components of God, in addition to three: 1) The Father, 2) The Son, and 3) The Holy Spirit. Again, seven (complete) plus three (perfect) equals ten (holiness). "God is complete perfect holiness." We will deal more with this when we get to the section on ten, but it is interesting that there are seven spirits within the trinity.

In an attempt to minimize the proof of seven, I will not go into great detail here, but briefly point out the designation and use of seven pertaining to the law and the Ten Commandments to convince you of the significance of seven.

In the process of ordaining a priest, there was a waiting period of seven days in order to be purified. Moses during this ceremony had to sprinkle blood seven times on the altar as part of the ceremony for the ordaining of a priest. Blood also had to be sprinkled on the mercy seat seven times as a sin offering. The seventh month was designated as the month for celebration of the Feast of Tabernacles, which lasted seven days and was to be a time for cleansing from sin.

Jews were to eat only unleavened bread during the seven days of Passover. The Feast of Weeks was to last for seven weeks. Note that they were to have three celebrations per year designated by God as part of the process to keep them "perfect and complete" as a chosen nation. All three celebrations include seven—seven days, seven weeks, or in the seventh month.

Remember in studying three that we learned the Lord chose Israel for His purpose in three ways. In Deuteronomy 4, we find seven additional ways God chose Israel: The first being by trials, 2) by signs, 3) by wonders, 4) by war, 5) with a mighty hand, 6) with an outstretched arm, and 7) by great terrors. We now have three ways plus seven ways in which God chose Israel. Again, three plus seven equals ten or "holiness"—a reference to God's call of holiness on Israel. He will make them a perfect and pure nation in the last days.

God gives us seven ways to show our love for Him: We are to fear Him, to walk in His ways, to love Him, to serve Him with all our heart, to serve Him with all our soul, to keep His Commandments, and to keep His ordinances. Deuteronomy 10 offers seven descriptions of God's character: He is the God of gods, Lord of lords, a great God, a mighty God, a terrible God, a God who does not take bribes, and our judge. **God tests us in seven ways to see if we love Him: we must love Him with all our heart, we must love Him with all our soul, we must fear Him, we must keep His Commandments, we must obey His voice, we must serve Him, and we must cleave to Him.**

Here is some trivia on numbers: there are three places designated for the sprinkling of blood seven times for the forgiveness of sin: the veil, the altar, and the mercy seat. It took seven years to build the temple. Satan attacked Job seven times. The promises of the Lord are purified seven times. Wisdom is built on seven pillars. Liars have seven abominations in their hearts. Jesus twice fed thousands of people with seven items of food and in one case had seven baskets left over and in another had twelve left over (this is another instance of numbers in numbers that are easily overlooked, but more on this when we get to twelve).

Let us break down the case of seven baskets by starting with the obvious, five loaves of bread plus two fish. Jesus represents seven, the sum of five plus two, complete, pure, the one to rest in. Five and two symbolize, "a sign to man who bore witness to God's completeness." The less obvious breakdown uses one plus six to equal seven, or "God as man equals completion and purification." Another formula breakdown in this case could be; two plus five, "a confirmed sign" that equals three plus four, or a "perfect judge, Jesus." These recorded events of feeding thousands of people used numbers to depict more than just the story of the miracles of Christ; they also revealed a message in a message.

Take note that Pilate approached the people seven times in hopes of releasing Jesus. The resurrection of Jesus was on the morning after the seventh day of the Jewish celebration of Passover. His resurrection was on the first day of the week. Luke tells us it was the day of preparation, the sixth day of the Passover that He was crucified and buried. To be interpreted as "a day the Savior died for man." Even today during the celebration of Passover on the sixth day, two candles are lit to symbolize the joy and the light God gives. It is hard to miss the symbolism of this event in the use of numbers. It is interesting to note that many Orthodox Jews now celebrate eight days of Passover, after all the resurrection was on the eighth day of Passover, more on this in section eight.

The seven spirits of God are mentioned four times in Revelation, and four represents judgment. Rather fitting, isn't it, that seven and four mean "complete and pure judgment" in the end?

Seven jumps out at you in Joshua. Joshua was told to take the Ark of the Covenant and march around Jericho once a day for six days with seven priests blowing seven trumpets. The people were not allowed to talk for seven days. On the seventh day, the Israelites marched around the walls of the city seven times. The trumpets blew, the people shouted, and the walls came down. The Israelites were told to destroy everything in the city, including all the people. In this way, God demonstrated the importance of seven for purification of His people; they were told to take nothing from the victory; if they did, they would defy themselves as a chosen people.

Ezekiel 39 declared seven as the number for cleansing; God uses this number to purify or to cleanse the world once again. The wrath of God will come upon all flesh due to seven sins: 1) the worship of things made by man, 2) murder, 3) sorcery, 4) immorality, 5) thievery (stealing tithes from God), 6) the worship of false gods and 7) the worship of demons. Ezekiel tells of seven kinds of destruction in the last days, seven nations to come against Israel, and the seven years the world will be led by the antichrist.

The book of Revelation contains four sets of seven referring to judgment. The first set of seven being the judgment upon four churches claiming to follow Jesus and the encouragement of the other three churches, referred to as the seven churches. Here if you took one times four, plus three equals seven, it would be understood as "God's judgment by perfection- equals' complete purity." After all, scriptures teach that judgment begins with the house of God. The church here is not a denomination necessarily, but believers proclaiming to follow Jesus, as a group and as individuals. The next three sets of seven refers to the judgment of the world including the church. There are seven seals, seven trumpets, and seven bowls of wrath. Remember that four represents judgment and seven-"purification, completion, or cleansing." If we take the number definitions of the individual numbers, and apply to the text within Revelation, we have seven and four, depicting God's wrath as "complete and pure judgment". Referring to the churches, with seven being the sum of three plus four: translated means, "God's perfect judgment on the church." The remaining three sets, (three of seven) symbolize "the perfect cleansing" of the world.

In the context of the seven churches are seven promises to those who overcome the world and persevere to the end, making them "complete and cleansed." The terminology to conquer or overcome the world is used five times in the King James Version; I believe this was stated to understand that the saints are to be a "sign" to the rest of the world. Four churches are called to repent or be judged with the rest of the world; the other three are called to be faithful, to be watchful, remember God and His works, to keep His Word, and to hold fast—five commands. Here again we see judgment represented by four and the perfect church by the designation of three. The perfect church is to live by five commands. This perfect church is not necessarily a denomination, but represents the saints. They are seen as "signs of perfect witness (five equals, three plus two)" to the alpha and the omega, the creator of all things, of God to those who are still living.

Note another set of seven within the seven seals, seven angels with seven trumpet blasts. With the sixth seal, seven things will be revealed in the end: a great earthquake, a darkened sun, a red moon, stars falling, sky disappearing, mountains and islands moving, and men realizing the wrath of God is upon them. Here in the context of the sixth seal upon man, the seventh significant event is that humanity acknowledges the complete wrath of God on mankind.

It is also interesting to note here that before judgment can begin, "one" must be found worthy of opening the seven seals designated for the time of judgment. None will be found except the Lamb of God, symbolically recognized with seven horns that represent the seven spirits, and seven eyes indicating, He sees everything "completely." He alone is the only "one" worthy of opening the scroll with seven seals designated for the end. Note the seven reasons He is worthy of opening the seals: The first was that He was slain to receive power and to redeem us by His blood, He is worthy of receiving riches, He is wisdom, He is strength, He is honor, He is glory, and blessings are His. Notice the counterfeit that shows up out of the sea with seven heads and with seven crowns compared to seven horns and seven eyes of Christ.

However, in the midst of all the doom and gloom, we can have the peace and comfort that comes with confidence and the assurance by being right with God. First, we must recognize the "one" God contains seven components of wisdom and truth that He gives us: purity, peace, gentleness, reason, full of mercy, producing good fruit and sincerity. In addition to these is another set of seven principles to dwell on, that which is true, honorable, just, pure, lovely, gracious, and excellent -worthy of praise.

Through Jesus, we are given seven articles of armor to fight the fight: we are to guard our loins with truth, put on the breastplate of righteousness, guide our feet with the gospel of peace, hold high the shield of faith, put on the helmet of salvation, wield the sword of the Spirit, which is the Word of God. The last one, the seventh one is to pray without ceasing, being led by the Spirit of God. God wants us to make use of the might, the power and the authority of God's Word that He has given to those that believe.

When we have finished the race, we will have the privilege of worshipping the Lord in seven ways: 1) with blessing, 2) with glory to Him, 3) For His wisdom, 4) with thanksgiving, 5) with knowing He is the only one deserving honor, 6) with respect for His power, 7) and with respect for His eternal might as God forever and ever.

Number Seven References

There are seven symbolic days to complete creation (Genesis 1–2).

God rested on the seventh day (Genesis 2).

Anyone seeking revenge on Cain would be punished sevenfold (Genesis 4).

Noah was in the ark for seven days before it started to rain (Genesis 7).

Seven pairs of clean animals were brought on the ark (Genesis 7).

It took seven days to load all the animals on the ark (Genesis 7).

The ark came to rest in the seventh month (Genesis 8).

Noah sent birds out three separate times, seven days apart to test for dry land (Genesis 8).

Note there are seven sets of seven regarding Noah and the flood (Genesis 7–8).

Jacob bargained for his wife for seven years. Then he worked another seven years after being tricked by his father-in-law; these two sets of seven could be defined as complete acknowledgement from God regarding his wife (Genesis 29).

Jacob bowed seven times to Esau upon seeing Esau once again (Genesis 33).

Pharaoh had two dreams each about seven (Genesis 41).

Moses married one of seven sisters (Exodus 2).

The Nile remained like blood for seven days (Exodus 7).

Seven days of eating unleavened bread are required for Passover (Exodus 12, 23).

While in the wilderness, no one was to gather bread sent by God on the seventh day (Exodus 23).

The seventh day was made for rest. We are to rest on it (Exodus 23, 31).

God called Moses to Mount Sinai on the seventh day after a cloud covered the mountain for six days (Exodus 24).

Seven lamp stands were to be placed in front of the Ark of the Covenant (Exodus 25).

Priests were to dip their fingers in the blood and sprinkle blood on the veil seven times for sin offerings (Leviticus 4).

Seven days were required to ordain a priest for purification (Leviticus 8).

When anointing the priests, Moses sprinkled the altar with blood seven times for priests; they were not allowed to leave the temple for seven days for purposes of purification (Leviticus 8).

Women were considered unclean for seven days after giving birth to a male. Remember that the woman was considered unclean for sixty-six days if she gave birth to a female (Leviticus 12).

Seven days were required after the birth of a male child before circumcision was to be performed on the eighth day (Leviticus 12).

Seven days were required to determine if someone had leprosy (Leviticus 13).

Priests were to sprinkle blood and oil seven times on lepers to cleanse them (Leviticus 13).

Seven days were required for cleansing (Leviticus 15).

Seven days were required before a young bull could be presented as a sin offering (Leviticus 16).

Blood was to be sprinkled seven times in three places for sin offerings: the veil, the altar, and the mercy seat (Leviticus 4, 8, 16; note the three sets of seven).

The seventh day of the week was to be kept holy (Leviticus 23).

Seven days were required for the Fast of Unleavened Bread (Leviticus 23).

Seven lambs were required for burnt offerings (Leviticus 23).

The seventh month was designated as the month of celebration. The Feast of Tabernacles was to last seven days. There was to be no work, for it was a time of cleansing from sin (Leviticus 16, 23).

Seven weeks of years were defined as seven times seven for harvest; the land was to rest during the fiftieth year (Leviticus 25; this designation in figurative speech is important later regarding prophecies in the last days by Daniel). The fiftieth year was the year of Jubilee.

God punished the Israelites sevenfold because of their sin (Leviticus 26).

Seven lamp stands were to be in front of the altar (Numbers 7).

A heifer was to be sacrificed and burned. The ashes were to be used to purify and make holy water. Anyone touching a dead person was unclean for seven days. He was to bath himself in holy water on the third and seventh day to become clean (Numbers 19).

Balaam made seven altars to the Lord three times. Each altar had seven bulls and seven rams for sacrifice. Balaam blessed Israel three times (Numbers 23).

Slaves were to be set free in the seventh year of slavery (Exodus 21).

God chose Israel by seven ways: 1) trials, 2) by signs, 3) by wonders, 4) by war, 5) by a mighty hand, 6) by an outstretched arm, and 7) great terrors (Deuteronomy 4).

We are to show our love for God in seven ways: by 1) fearing Him, 2) walking in His ways, 3) love Him, 4) serve the Lord with all your heart and 5) serving Him with all our soul, 6) keeping His Commandments, and 7) keeping His statues (Deuteronomy 10).

There were seven nations greater and stronger than Israel that were to be given to them by the Lord upon defeating their armies. God commands that all must be destroyed and to make no covenant with them. They were not to take any women as wives and to show no mercy. If they disobeyed, God's anger would be upon them, for they are chosen to be a Holy nation (Deuteronomy 7).

Seven descriptions of God's character: 1) God of gods, 2) Lord of lords, 3) a great God, 4) a mighty God, 5) a God to be feared, 6) an incorruptible God and 7) He is the God of judgment (Deuteronomy 10).

Seven ways to apply His principles (Deuteronomy 11).

Seven directions on giving to the Lord (Deuteronomy 12).

God tests our love for Him in seven ways: Do we love Him with all our heart? With all our soul? Do we fear Him? Do we keep His Commandments? Do we obey His voice? Do we serve him? Do we cleave to Him? (Deuteronomy 13).

Debts were forgiven after seven years (Deuteronomy 15).

During their three celebrations, there was no eating of leavened bread for seven days. The Feast of Weeks was to last for seven weeks. Passover and the Feast of Tabernacles were each to last seven days. This was required from God for the purpose of "perfecting (three) the purification process to completion (seven)" of the Jewish people (Deuteronomy 16, Ezekiel 44–45).

Ezekiel is overwhelmed for seven days and fed by the birds (Ezekiel 3).

The enemies of Israel would flee in seven ways if Israel obeyed God (Deuteronomy 28).

Every seven years, the laws were to be read at the Feast of Tabernacles (Deuteronomy 31).

Seven priests walked before the ark with seven trumpets at Jericho. For six days, they circled Jericho. Then on the seventh day, they circled Jericho seven times and blew seven trumpets. The people were not allowed to talk during the seven days (Joshua 6).

There were seven tribes of Israel even after many years of war that did not receive their inheritance due to their disobedience (Joshua 18).

It took seven years to build the temple (1 Kings 6).

The famine during David's time lasted seven years (1 Kings 8).

Elisha spread himself over a young boy who dies. The boy sneezes seven times and comes back to life (2 Kings 4).

Elisha told Naaman to wash seven times in the Jordan to cure his leprosy (2 Kings 5).

Ishmael was born in the seventh month (2 Kings 25).

Solomon dedicated the temple in the seventh month (2 Chronicles 6).

The celebration of the temple's completion lasted seven days (2 Chronicles 7).

Job was attacked by Satan seven times (Job 2).

The promises of the Lord are purified seven times (Psalm 12).

David praised the Lord seven times a day (Psalm 119).

The Lord hates seven abominable sins: pride, lying, shedding innocent blood, wickedness of heart, following mischief, bearing false witness, and spreading discord (Proverbs 6).

Wisdom is built on seven pillars (Proverbs 9).

A righteous man may fall seven times but will rise again (Proverbs 24).

Liars have seven abominations in their hearts (Proverbs 26).

Judah is guilty of seven sins: greed, self-indulgence, materialism, sexual perversion, pride, drunkenness, and lack of integrity (Isaiah 5).

There are seven spirits of the Lord: 1) the Spirit of the Lord, 2) the Spirit of wisdom, 3) the Spirit of understanding, 4) the Spirit of counsel, 5) the Spirit of might, 6) the Spirit of knowledge, and 7) the Spirit of the fear of the Lord (Isaiah 11).

The tongue of the sea of Egypt (between the Red Sea and Mediterranean Sea) will be split into seven streams which man will be able to walk across in the last days (Isaiah 11–12).

Leviathan, a demon prince of seven spirits, will be destroyed in the end (Isaiah 27).

In that day (the latter days), the sun will be seven times hotter (Isaiah 30).

The Lord will call out for seven (six plus one) destroyers in the end (Ezekiel 9).

The Lord will bring seven kinds of destruction in the last days, and seven nations will come against Israel. Israel will be attacked from the north (Ezekiel 38).

Israel will burn the weapons used against them in the end times for seven years; it takes seven months to bury the dead (Ezekiel 39).

Seven signifies cleansing (Ezekiel 39).

On the seventh day of each month, sin offerings were to be made with seven bulls and rams (Ezekiel 44–45).

Daniel described the image of a man from the king's dream with seven details (Daniel 2).

There were three men thrown into a furnace burning seven times hotter than ever (Daniel 3).

There is a covenant for many during the last seven years (Daniel 9).

Daniel had fasted for three weeks (seven days a week) when Gabriel delivered a message about the last days; notice the three sets of seven in the context (Daniel 10). This is also a great passage revealing spiritual warfare.

Seven lamps are in front of God's throne (Zechariah 4).

Seven shepherds and one other (eight men total) will go up against the antichrist. Here is another insight of numbers within numbers. Why was it stated this way and not just eight men in the first place? (Micah 5).

Those freed of demons that are not filled with the Spirit of God will be seven times worse (Matthew 12, Luke 11).

Jesus twice fed thousands of people with seven items of food and in one case had seven baskets left over (Matthew 15).

We are to forgive others seven times seventy times (Matthew 18).

Seven demons were cast out of Mary Magdalene (Mark 16, Luke 7–8).

Jesus was circumcised and named on the eighth day after seven days of purification (Luke 2).

Pilate approached the people seven times in hopes of releasing Jesus (John 18–19).

Seven were selected for leadership in the church (Acts 6).

Seven sons of a priest attempted an exorcism and the demon beat them all up and left them naked (Acts 19).

We are to arm ourselves in seven ways for spiritual battle: 1) we are to guard our loins with truth, 2) put on the breastplate of righteousness, 3) guide our feet with the gospel of peace, 4) carry the shield of faith, 5) wear the helmet of salvation, 6) wield the sword of the Spirit, the Word of God and 7) be praying continuously in the Spirit (Ephesians 6).

Seven principles to dwell on, that which is true, honorable, just, pure, lovely, gracious, and excellent and worthy of praise (Philippians 4).

God's wisdom has seven attributes: it is pure, peaceful, gentle, reasonable, merciful, produces good fruit and is sincere (James 3).

Seven churches are mentioned in Revelation (2-3).

Seven spirits of God sit before His throne (Revelation 1).

Seven lamp stands, seven stars, and seven angels are before God's throne (Revelation 1). Note the three sets of seven.

The physical appearance of Jesus is described in seven ways (Revelation 1).

Seven promises exist for those who overcome the world (Revelation 1–4).

Before the throne are seven torches, the seven spirits of God (Revelation 1, 3, 4).

The Lamb of God, with seven horns and seven eyes, is the only one worthy of opening the scroll with seven seals (Revelation 5).

Jesus alone is worthy in seven ways to open the seals: He was slain to receive power thereby redeeming us with His blood, He alone is worthy to receive riches, He is wisdom, He is strength, He is honor, He is glory, and He is worthy of blessing (Revelation 5).

The sixth seal reveals seven things in the end: a great earthquake, a darkened sun, a red moon, stars falling from the sky, the sky disappearing, mountains and islands are removed from their place, and men realizing the wrath of God is upon them (Revelation 6).

The Lord eternally is worshipped in seven ways: with blessing, glory, wisdom, thanksgiving, honor, power, and might (Revelation 7).

Remember the first set of four sets of seven, is the judgment of the church in the first three chapters of Revelation; judgment begins in the house of the Lord first. Then three sets of seven events of judgment upon the world with seven angels, seven seals, and seven trumpets (Revelation 8).

There are seven sins man does not repent of: 1) the worship of things made by man, 2) murder, 3) sorcery, 4) immorality, 5) thievery or stealing tithes from God, 6) the worship of false gods and 7) the worship of demons (Revelation 9).

John heard seven thunders he was not allowed to write or repeat (Revelation 10).

Two beasts appear out of the sea with seven heads; one with seven crowns (Revelation 12–13).

Seven angels, with seven plagues, and seven bowls of wrath will come in the latter days (Revelation 15).

The seventh angel poured his bowl into the air, and a voice came from the throne saying, "It is finished." Four things appear, lightning, voices, thunder, and the largest earthquake ever destroying everything (Revelation 16).

A female demon, "Babylon" by name, will sit on the beast with seven heads (seven kings) and seven mountains, and ten horns (Revelation 17).

One of seven angels showed John the New Jerusalem with a great wall around it. There are twelve gates, facing four directions with three angels at each gate

(Revelation 21). Note the sum of four sets of three equals seven depicting "perfect judgment." If you multiply three times four you get twelve depicting "God's authority inside the gates." The total number of angels at the gates equal thirty six. This would be understood as three times ten plus six; or "perfect holiness of man inside the gates." Can you see the significance of numbers within the numbers, within the context? By the way, twelve means "authority." In this case symbolizing God's authority at the gates of the New Jerusalem.

NOTES

Section Eight

The Number Eight

Eight means being set apart or chosen for God, to be made an example of.
Noah and seven others were saved or set apart from the wrath of God upon the earth. Remember all the sevens involved in the redemption of Noah? God made a covenant with Abraham that all male children were to be named and circumcised on the eighth day after birth, after seven days of purification. Circumcision "set the Jews apart" from other cultures and other people. We are told in the New Testament that believers are to dwell on eight things and have eight characteristics that set them apart from the rest of the world. Jesus named eight characteristics of unbelievers that will set them apart from those in heaven. Jesus rose from the dead on the eighth day of Passover. Even today, some Jews celebrate Passover for eight days defining this extra day as an extra day of holiness.

Number Eight References

Eight people were saved in Noah's ark (Genesis 6–7).

Males were to be circumcised on the eighth day, as a "sign" that they are separated and are to be a chosen people, "set apart" from other nations (Genesis 17).This sign is demonstrated in eight as five plus three, "a sign of perfection that equals being set apart."

Male children were to be circumcised on the eighth day, after seven days of purification (Leviticus 12).

A leper that had been healed was to celebrate on the eighth day (Leviticus 14).

Two birds were to be offered as a sin offering on the eighth day (Leviticus 15).

Animals designated for sacrifice must stay with their mothers seven days; on the eighth day, they could be sacrificed (Leviticus 22).

The Lord used a set of eight ways to set Israel apart from other nations. For what nation has been 1) chosen out of another nation by 2) trials, 3) by signs,4) by wonders, 5) by war, 6) a mighty hand,7) and a outstretched arm, 8) and great terrors from Egypt (Deuteronomy 4:34). This indicates the significance of "being set apart" from Egypt, selected out of Egypt by including the eighth way.

David was the eighth son of Jesse and anointed to be king (1 Samuel 16).

On the eighth day, priests will make burnt and peace offerings in the New Jerusalem (Ezekiel 43).

When the antichrist from Syria tramples Israel and Judah, seven religious leaders plus one will go against him (Micah 5).

John the Baptist was named and circumcised on the eighth day after his birth (Luke 1).

Jesus was named and circumcised on the eighth day after His birth (Luke 2).

Noah was the eighth soul saved from the flood (1 Peter 3, 2 Peter 2).

Believers are to dwell on eight things setting them apart from nonbelievers: that which is 1) truthful, 2) what is honorable and honest, 3) what is just, 4) whatever is pure, 5) whatever is lovely, 6) whatever is gracious, 7) virtuous, and 8) worthy of praise (Philippians 4). These characteristics set the follower of Christ apart from the rest of the world.

Those with the wisdom of God have eight qualities: they are 1) pure, 2) they are peaceful, 3) they are gentle, 4) reasonable, 5) full of mercy, 6) produce good fruits, 7) without partiality and 8) not hypocritical (James 3). They are to be "set apart" from others.

God provides the fountain of water for life, to those who thirst for Him; For the other eight types of people, the cowardly, the faithless, the polluted, the murderers, the fornicators, the sorcerers, the idolaters, and the liars-will end up in the lake of fire that burns with sulfur (Revelation 21).

Section Nine

The Number Nine

Nine is used in the Old Testament to refer mostly to periods, referring to age, or a specific period of time, day, month or hour. It is also symbolic of preparation for "holiness," or number ten. In Leviticus, for instance, the ninth day was specified as a day of preparation for the tenth, the Day of Atonement, a time for people to prepare for atonement of their sin. The prophets referred to nine when Israel is destroyed several times. Jesus died in the ninth hour of the day, after six hours of hanging on the cross. His death symbolizing a time of "preparation unto Holiness" (number ten). Jesus' death in the ninth hour could symbolize numbers within a number, in this case three plus six equals nine, "a perfect man's death to prepare for holiness." His death could also be understood as three sets of three whose sum is nine; the first of three hours on the cross, the second set of three hours of darkness on the cross and three days in the tomb. These nine periods were preparation unto holiness.

Number Nine References

The ninth day and evening was to be a day of preparing for the tenth, the Day of Atonement, before God, It was to be like a Sabbath day (Leviticus 23).

For six years, the Israelites were to eat the fresh fruit supplied by the Lord. For the next three years, they were to eat the dried fruit (nine years total, Leviticus 25). Here are two numbers with a sum of nine, six plus three, or "man (Israel) being perfected in preparation for holiness."

The king of Babylon destroyed Judah and Jerusalem in the ninth month (Jeremiah 36).

In the ninth year of Zedekiah's reign, the king of Babylon overtook Jerusalem. In the ninth day of the eleventh year and fourth month, Jerusalem was breached and Zedekiah's eyes were poked out and he was led off to Babylon (Jeremiah 39).

There was darkness that came over all the land from the sixth until the ninth hour, (for three hours) when Jesus was crucified; Jesus was crucified on the third hour. He died in the ninth hour (Matthew 27, Luke 23).

Once when Jesus was in Jerusalem ten lepers came and cried out for mercy. He told them to go see the chief priest. On their way, they are healed. One comes back and gives thanks to Jesus and Jesus asks where are the other nine? The one that returned was made whole by his faith (Luke 17).

Nine qualities characterize the fruit of the Spirit: 1) love, 2) joy, 3) peace, 4) patience, 5) kindness, 6) goodness, 7) faithfulness, 8) gentleness and 9) self control (Galatians 5). One breakdown among several could be this; look at these as eight plus one equals nine, or "those set apart by God, in preparation for holiness." If you used three times three, equals nine; being interpreted as the "saints are being perfected and confirmed unto holiness." More on this later.

Section Ten

The Number Ten

Ten represents holiness, power, and or righteousness. This was first demonstrated with the ten miracles God performed to free the Israelites from Pharaoh's control. God gave Ten Commandments to the people to make them righteous as the chosen people. There were ten curtains required on the inside of the Tent of Meeting to cover the Ark of the Covenant. This indicated the holiness of the law and the ark.

The Israelites were not to work during the tenth month to cleanse them from sin and make them holy. The temple of God was to be considered so holy that a child from a spouse that was non- Jewish could not enter the temple, even to the tenth generation. In the latter days, only one out of ten Jews will be alive as of the result of God's wrath upon them. Jeremiah recognized he needed ten days to know the will of God. Satan's counterfeit will appear with ten kings and ten kingdoms.

In Revelation, John described the physical appearance of Christ with ten physical descriptions that reflected His holiness.

How can God have three components, the Father, the Son, and Holy Spirit, and also contain or coexist with seven spirits of God as "one"? Putting this into a formula; the sum of three, plus seven, equaling ten; ten being symbolic for "holiness, power and righteousness." The Holy Spirit is composed of the seven spirits that complete the Trinity. The numbers define God as a "God that is composed of perfect and complete holiness." The sum makes the whole.

By making a formula of the basic ten numbers, times ten, which represents holiness, you will see how understanding each number defines the next number within the number. It all starts at the beginning with number "one." Here the product makes the whole.

- 1 times 10 equals God of holiness or God of gods, all-powerful, all righteous.
- 2 times 10 equals confirmed holiness
- 3 times 10 equals perfect holiness, perfect power
- 4 times 10 equals judgment by holiness and righteousness
- 5 times 10 equals a sign of, for, or by holiness
- 6 times 10 equals man's rejection of holiness

- 7 times 10 equals complete holiness, complete power, complete righteousness.
- 8 times 10 equals being set apart for holiness
- 9 times 10 equals a time to prepare for holiness
- 10 times 10 equals holiness confirmed

Number Ten References

Ten miracles through Moses in Egypt were demonstrated, before the Pharaoh lets Israel go (Exodus 7–10).

The first writing of the Ten Commandments (Exodus 20, Deuteronomy 5).

The Lord designated to have ten curtains inside the temple as a covering over the Ark of the Covenant (Exodus 26).

The second writing of the Ten Commandments (Exodus 34).

During the tenth month, Israelites were not to work as a cleansing for sin (Leviticus 16).

The tenth day of the seventh month was to be a time for atonement (Leviticus 23).

Israel tempted the Lord ten times and chose not to obey Him (Numbers 14).

Ten of the twelve spies sent to Canaan came back with negative reports and died of a plague. Note only two (witnesses) came back with a positive report. They were the only two that entered into the promise land out of all of Israel. These two were the only ones that trusted in God (Numbers 14).

A non-Jewish or half-Jewish child was not to enter into the temple even to the tenth generation (Deuteronomy 23).

After three woes upon Israel in the last days, only one-tenth of the Jews will remain (Isaiah 6).

It took ten days for Jeremiah to learn the will of God (Jeremiah 42).

Daniel and three companions proved their diet to be better than the others in ten days (Daniel 1).

The image that Daniel describes of Nebuchadnezzar's dream is of a man with ten toes (Daniel 2).

The king of the fourth and last kingdom, symbolically named "Babylon" will have ten horns or ten kings backing him up (Daniel 7).

Only a tenth of Jews will remain in the last days (Amos 5).

Ten lepers healed by Jesus and only one returns to give thanks (Luke 17).

In a parable told by Jesus, ten servants were given ten pounds (a symbolic measure of worth) as a reward for their investment in the kingdom of God (Luke 19).

This is symbolic in that they are given something of value and precious. These servants are given holiness and wisdom from God. The message here is a question; what are we investing in, money or the kingdom of God?

Have you ever questioned whether or not you are saved? There are ten assurances that we must ask ourselves to know with confidence where we stand regarding our salvation found in I John. 1) We must choose to walk in the light, not in darkness, choosing not to follow evil. 2) We must confess that we are sinners and confess our sin. 3) We are to keep His commandments and His words. 4) We choose not to follow the world, and stand against the ways of the world. 5) We acknowledge that Jesus is the son of God, our Savior and our Christ. 6) We love one another in deed and in truth, not just in deed. 7) We abide in him. 8) We do that which is righteous. 9) We do the will of God and lastly 10) we hope in His return.

John described the person speaking to him with ten qualities: 1) like the Son of Man, 2) clothed in a long robe, 3) a golden girdle around his chest, with 4) white hair, and 5) eyes like a flaming fire. He goes on to describe His 6) feet are like bronze, 7) having a voice like the sound of many waters, 8) He is holding seven stars in His right hand, 9) He holds a two edged sword in His mouth and 10) His face was shining like the sun (Revelation 1).

Some believers will be thrown into prison for ten days in the last days (Revelation 2); this is a time designated for the saints to be "a sign and bear witness to God's holiness." This is understood by the formula of five, times two, equals ten.

The beast with ten horns that represent ten kings is explained (Revelation 12).

The beast with ten horns and ten crowns is dealt with (Revelation 13).

The ten horns are ten kings who receive their power for one hour with the beast. They all turn their power and authority over to the beast for a common purpose. They will make war with the Lamb, but the lamb wins and the chosen are with the lamb (Revelation 17).

Interesting Notes on Ten

We are told twice (confirmation) that only a tenth of the people of Israel and Judah will remain in the last days. This is the "remnant" of Israel mentioned by the prophets as a judgment on them for disobedience.

NOTES

Section Eleven

Symbolism

God consistently uses symbolism within events, people and numbers. They constantly intertwine together and we miss so much when we do not recognize these messages within the message. To further demonstrate the numeric symbolism God uses to teach man, let's look at the symbolic act of circumcision, which was to occur on the eighth day after the birth of males. They were also to be named on the eighth day. Isn't it a bit odd that the Creator required men to be circumcised? Why did He not just make them that way from the beginning? Why would God require a man's penis to be circumcised as a covenant between God and man? I don't mean to be crude here, but I do want to point out the significance of the symbolism.

One must consider the physical facts to understand their spiritual significance and symbolism. Circumcision involves an area that is biologically in the center of men. That "area" is also what men center on.

I'm sure every man has been asked in reference to sex, "Is that all you ever think about?" God created the penis for removing waste, for pleasure, and for reproduction. Though it is a private area hidden by clothing, it is used every day. Men generally have a sense of pride about their "tools," which are naturally made with an excess of flesh. When the flesh is removed by circumcision, the penis becomes more sensitive. Circumcision also assists in cleanliness. Circumcision comes from the word *circumscribe*, meaning to encircle, or to be centered on something.

Abraham was a man chosen by God to create a nation of people that God could bless and make an example of. The Lord chose circumcision as a sign for this nation to be set apart for God, to be clean and spiritually more sensitive; to be centered on Him. He did this to make the Israelites an example of what happens to those who obey or disobey God. Abraham was the first required by God to be circumcised. Every male of his descendants thereafter were to be circumcised on the eighth day, the day to be "set apart" from all other tribes, nations and men.

Looking at the spiritual implications of circumcision, it is meant for one who loves and seeks God, as Abraham did. By removal of the flesh, it symbolizes the removal of the sinful ways of man, the "flesh". After all what do men center on? What is driving them, self-pleasure? Or are you centered upon the reproduction of a spiritual man. To bring forth fruit, if you will, of the spirit of God. As to getting rid of waste, we are wretched in the sight of the Lord; we are nothing but waste because of the flesh. Yet if we center on God and let ourselves be surrounded (circumscribed) by God, we can be clean and our impurities can be washed away. We can even increase our spiritual sensitivity toward God. As men daily use their penises, they can be reminded who they are, what they center on, and how their thoughts are directed as to the use of their tool, not the physical "tool", but the spiritual tool God has given them, that being the sword or the word of God.

Some questions all of us who are men should ask ourselves can sometimes be rather revealing of our true selves. Are our thoughts on our tools, or the tools given by the Spirit? Are our thoughts perverted or holy? What do we do in our secret lives hidden from others? Are we seeking pleasure or God? What are we driven by? Are we willing to go through the pain of the removal of the flesh? Being circumcised is a constant reminder that we believers are to be set apart, chosen to be holy, encircled by God, and having him as the center of our lives. It is an area hidden to men but known by God. In the same way, our hearts are hidden to man, but known by God. Jesus stated that our hearts had to be circumcised. The symbolism of the act is revealed in that statement.

If we put this act of circumcision into a formula then we can recognize the symbolism within the act thus increasing our understanding. Here are several ways to break it down. Three represents "perfection," and five is "a sign for man"; their sum is eight. Circumcision is a "perfect sign that equals being set apart for God" and being centered on Him. What if we broke it down as six plus two? "Man's confirmation to be set apart for God." Or one plus seven, "God purging a nation by separating them from others." Another one could be, four plus four-"judgment confirmed upon the Jews."

Jesus used symbolism within symbolism many times. When Jesus referred to mankind as having circumcised hearts, He was referring to mankind, women included. He made it apparent He was talking about the flesh, our hidden sinful nature that needs to be removed so we might be clean before Him.

Physically the penis can get excited and rise in response to fleshly desires. God wants us to be excited, if you will, about Him and rise against the flesh. As we go through life, we are daily reminded of the need for removal of the flesh through the death of Jesus to cleanse us, and set us apart for God. A physical act, symbolically referring to a spiritual condition; thus, the revealing of the symbolism of our hearts to be circumcised, or symbolism within symbolism.

Why does God speak with symbolism? Why is He not just direct? God does not always give us direct answers pertaining to His ways; this is why Jesus spoke in parables and the prophets described strange visions. I believe He speaks this way to challenge us to seek Him so we may understand His truth and nature. He wants us to seek Him with our hearts, minds, and souls. He wants us to search for Him, like a hidden treasure, to search for the mystery of God, to be enchanted with knowing Him, to hunger and thirst after Him.

Another example of His divine order in the usage of numbers is in His creation of water. The formula for water is H_2O. It is interesting to note that the source of life is made of three elements. I think this was not an accident but symbolic of God. You have two identical hydrogen atoms (Jesus and God) linked with one oxygen (the Holy Spirit) atom completing the formula to make water, the source of life. This is symbolic of the three elements of God, the Father, the Son, and the Holy Spirit. God is our source, our river of life.

Water is also used for cleansing, note the cleansing symbolism of water in baptism, and the cleansing of the world God performed with the flood. The next time, soon, He will purge the world with fire.

Oxygen is an element separate from hydrogen; it is in the air, just as the Holy Spirit is referred to as wind, Oxygen gives us breath; when Adam was created, God breathed life into him from His Spirit. Even in creation, God is a God of order and awe. If the truth could be known, I am sure there would be uncountable usage of repeated numbers in God's universe, for He does nothing by accident. Can you see the symbolism in His creation? It is by design that we cannot survive life without water or oxygen. Neither can we have life without God, who is comprised of three components linked to make one.

NOTES

Section Twelve

Numbers within Numbers

We must first be aware that the number system God created is based on one through ten. Every other number is composed of numbers within the numbers, a message within a message. We have seen a few of these situations previously in this study, and now we are delving further into the mysteries of God. They are sometimes hard to grasp, let alone define because we have to look at a number as well as its meaning within the number. Most often, a formula has to be developed. It is necessary to break down the message within the context using the definitions of numbers one thru ten. We have to let God out of the box, so to speak. Bear with me here; this section will hopefully help you understand any number in the Bible.

First, a little review, Jesus was crucified on the sixth day of the Passover celebration at the third hour. He died six hours later in the ninth hour, and buried in the last few moments of that day. Symbolically, by hanging on the cross for six hours, His death represented "death for man." Notice the set of two sixes in the context "confirming His death for man." He was crucified on the sixth day of Passover, and he was on the cross for six hours.

Regarding His time of death, the ninth hour, nine can be broken down with several formulas. Seven plus two equals "completion or purification confirmed," eight plus one equals being "set apart for God," three plus six equals "the perfect man," five plus four equals a "sign of judgment", and three, plus three, plus three equals "perfection stacked on perfection." The sum equaling the whole "perfect man, perfect salvation, perfect God." This could also symbolize the number of perfection, 333, all referring to Jesus and the act of being crucified in relationship to the timing of His death. All these formulas work within the context.

Regardless of how you break down the numbers, they reveal the nature of God or the act of God in reference to the context. He rose from the dead on the third day to be made perfect; was this accidental? I think not.

You will have to admit there is something peculiar about the use of specific numbers in Scriptures and symbolism about His death within the numbers and messages in messages. Jesus was on the cross for two sets of time, each containing a three-hour period; this could be translated as two times three, equals six, or "confirmed perfection of man." Remember too, that the last set of three hours was

73

the final designated time for the perfect temptation of a pure man without the Father's presence, who perfectly overcame the "perfect temptation."(For review on this go back to section three).

Sometimes we have to add numbers and other times multiply them, depending on the context or use of a number in a particular passage. In defining the meaning of numbers in English, we can sometimes add prepositions such as *-of, for, upon, in, to, as,* and other words to help clarify the meaning. One formula of numbers can also equal a different formula such as three plus seven can equal one times ten. This being translated as "perfect completion that equals a God of holiness."

This is where it gets awesome. To understand and grasp number relationships in the Word of God, this must be understood. There are numbers within numbers, and each is significant, but they all start with "one" and build off of it. Isn't that just like God that all things begin with Him, the "I am, the first and the last"? He is also the author within or contained if you will in each number. In other words His purpose, His Word relating to numbers, reflect back to Him by design. This reflection back on him is not by accident, but by a master design. God is a God of order and creation, including numbers. God deliberately used certain numbers and made sure they were recorded because they are part of His Word—His numbers are as important as His words and they too should be recognized, as the Word of God. Understanding this basic truth, allows us to study numbers within numbers and see how fascinating it is to discover their relationship to each other. Some numbers have similar meanings, but differ according to their uses in the context of the Scriptures, upon breaking them down, somehow they still work. It is possible that some definitions might be stretched, or are they?

By now, it should be obvious that Scriptures are full of numbers described by two or three other numbers, which God used to reveal His divine character and sometimes hidden messages to mankind. Many numbers are the sum of two or more numbers. Daniel referred to the last seventy years as sixty-two plus seven; I know this by itself does not equal seventy. However, it does demonstrate God using two numbers within the prophecy, a formula or breakdown with designated numbers. There must be a reason the Lord specifies numbers in this manner. Revelation is full of breakdowns of numbers in the seven-year period of tribulation, particularly the first and second three and-a-half-year periods, which incidentally have the sum of seven. Micah 5 refers to seven men plus one man (eight) to come against the antichrist. Christ's crucifixion includes a set of two three-hour periods. As you study the Scriptures, you will see that numbers are within numbers frequently. This is bizarre and yet astonishing and surprisingly consistent.

When you break down numbers you will find they apply to the reference being looked at; you will see numbers in numbers and some of the mysteries of God revealed.

Consider the number 1,000, referring to when Samson killed a thousand men with the jawbone of a donkey. You will see that any function of ten, such as ten times ten, is translated as "holiness stacked on holiness or holiness confirmed." Ten times ten, times ten, equals perfect holiness by the use of ten three times, and can be defined as "perfect power, perfect righteousness" within this passage found in Judges 15. Here God used Samson to kill the Philistines to fulfill God's holiness.

When it is mentioned that seven thousand men will be saved during Israel's last days, this would represent and be understood as a reference to these men being "complete in perfect holiness;" seven times a thousand, with the three zeros reflecting perfection. Sometimes there may be several ways of recording numbers with the same meaning or a slightly different perspective. The angel that Zechariah saw, asked the Lord, "How long will Jerusalem be punished for in the last days?" The Lord responded with the answer, "sixty plus ten years" or seventy years. Why did He not just say seventy years in the first place? Can you see that God had a message within the message by the use of the numbers being broken down? It is a time of "man against God's holiness (sixty), with God's holiness (ten) will equal complete and pure holiness (seventy)." You could also break down the number seventy in the following way; three plus four, times ten equals seventy or "perfect judgment by holiness, results in complete holiness." Totally appropriate referring to the end times (Zechariah 1:12).

The next couple of pages are perfect examples of numbers within numbers and recognizing the definitions within the word of God. There are many more symbolic messages within these verses and passages, however in an attempt to keep it simple, I will use only the most obvious.

In the book of Revelation, using the original King James Version, singing occurs in heaven after certain events. In chapters 2 & 3 of Revelation, the warning to the churches is to be right before the Lord, to stand firm in our faith, to stand with perseverance, that we may not lose our inheritance from the Lord.

After the seven churches have been chastised, John hears singing (Revelation 4). This is at the beginning of the seven-year tribulation where the singers are recognizing the worthiness of God to receive **three** qualities **1) glory, 2) honor**

and 3) power. These three qualities for worthiness are mentioned throughout Revelation, with other qualities being added intermittently as we will discover.

In Revelation 5, there is a book with seven seals revealed and no one is worthy to look at it or open it, except the Lamb of God-Jesus. He appears in the vision as a lamb that was slain, having seven eyes and seven horns. When the Lamb took the book, all heaven rejoiced and sang a new song for the Lamb was worthy in **seven** ways. For He and He alone is worthy of **1) power, 2) riches, 3) wisdom, 4) strength, 5) honor, 6) glory, and 7) blessing.**

Then in the next verse, still in chapter five, every creature which is in heaven and on earth, even under the sea sings **four** qualities to the lamb, **1) blessings, 2) honor, 3) glory and 4) power** belong to the Lamb.

First note the conditions of worthiness in Revelation 4 & 5 mentioned above; there are a total of **seven words** or descriptions of worthiness, some being repeated in the groupings. They are **glory, honor, power, riches, wisdom, strength, and blessing "describing complete worthiness."**

Next, looking at these "groupings" of the words within the text, you can understand the meaning of the numbers. First there is a group of three qualities, then seven, then four. This is to be understood as, "the lamb is worthy, for He is perfect and complete to judge." The third thing to notice is; **honor, glory and power** are repeated three times. This is to be interpreted as the "perfect glory, perfect honor, and perfect power" that the Lamb is worthy of.

The fourth item to be noticed is the word **blessing** being used in **two** groupings. Next note the additional words **riches, wisdom and strength** each being mentioned once comprising of another grouping. These three additional individual words are "perfect" additional qualities; riches, wisdom and strength. Remembering that glory, honor and power are also in each of these two other groupings. Now putting the numbers all together in these two chapters is to be interpreted as the Lamb is worthy; for "He is perfect glory, perfect honor, perfect power; He is complete with perfect riches, wisdom and strength, witnessed to by blessings, and worthy to be, the pure and perfect judge." In short the seven words previously mentioned, reveal the "perfect, complete, confirmed worthiness of God to judge." These parts are yet to make the whole, in the following chapters.

Next in chapter six of Revelation, the Lamb opens six seals. Then in chapter seven, John sees an angel delivering a message to four other angels to hold back on their destruction of the earth until the 144,000 received a seal from God upon their foreheads. After this, a great multitude which could not be counted, stood in white robes. They and the creatures sing out **seven** qualities of worthiness **1) blessing, 2) and glory, 3) and wisdom, 4) and thanksgiving, 5) and honor, 6), and power, 7) and might be unto God** forever and ever. Notice **five** descriptions are repeated; these being, blessing, glory, honor, power and wisdom. Then two new words are added, thanksgiving and might to complete this fourth group or set.

In Revelation 18 and 19, Babylon the terrible of nations is destroyed in one hour. For this nation has corrupted the earth and killed the saints of the Lord. Here the marriage supper of the Lamb is revealed. After the destruction of Babylon, **four** qualities are mentioned as the people in heaven sing **1) salvation, 2) glory, 3) honor and 4) power unto the Lord God.** Notice the group of the repeated three, and a fourth quality, the word salvation added to this fifth group of qualities for worthiness.

Now let us look at the numbers; **glory, honor and power,** three words are mentioned all five times. To be interpreted as a "perfect sign" of the worthiness of the Lamb of God, another message within the message. Three times the word **"blessing"** is used, which makes another perfect set or group of three meaning, "He is perfect in blessing." We now have six groups of three. Taking these six groups, plus a group of six additional words **Wisdom, riches, strength, thanksgiving, might and salvation** and adding them all together, we now have a total of twelve qualities of worthiness, revealing "His authority." Are you starting to see the message within the message?

Next taking the numbers of the qualities of Gods worthiness, in the order in which they appear throughout Revelation, we would have, 3, 7, 4, 7, and 4. Referring to the number of qualifications mentioned in each passage. A little review here; in Revelation 4 & 5 at the beginning of the seven-year tribulation, singing about the Lord's worthiness is heard. Three perfect characteristics are mentioned three times: glory, honor and power.

Then we see those in white robes after being sealed by the Spirit of God and seven "complete" characteristics are mentioned, in which glory, honor and power is again repeated. Then we see Babylon destroyed and again four characteristics revealing the Lambs' worthiness to "judge the world," this time salvation is included with glory, honor and power. Note that "blessings" were mentioned twice before the wrath of God fully begins. Next, we see the marking of the saints and seven characteristics are sung of the Lamb representing the saints to be "purified and complete." In the last passage are four reasons of worthiness depicting Him as a "worthy judge."

Here is where it gets awesome; to understand this completely it must be noted there are six sets, each containing three qualifications of worthiness of Christ. As we have noted, some of the words within the context have been repeated for the purpose of emphasizing the message within the numbers. Remember in sections three and six that there are six sets of three describing the counterfeit Christ, the anti-Christ. The difference between the two, is in the seventh set or group of the Lamb that the Lord reveals through numbers. This seventh group consists of the six remaining individual characteristics. The six remaining qualities are to be recognized as a formula, six being the product of three times two. This being interpreted as the "seventh complete and perfect confirmation" testifying to the worthiness of the Lamb. **The six words being; wisdom, riches, strength, thanksgiving, might, and salvation**. If you take all the words on an individual basis, without counting the repetition of words, there are **ten words, along with seven groups of words that describe the worthiness of the Lamb as "complete holiness ."** Fascinating isn't it? The sum of all the qualifications, making the whole! The seventh group identifying the real Christ from the anti-Christ. Jesus is the message of the numbers within the numbers, He is indeed worthy!

"Diggin' Deeper"

Let's review the first numbers to observe that there are numbers in numbers even with the basic numbers. **"One" is where we start—God's number.** All creation comes from Him. It all starts with God. The first of the Ten Commandments-have no other gods before him. He is to be recognized as the only God.

Two represents to bear witness, testify, or acknowledge a fact, a confirmation. It is the sum of one plus one, God bearing witness to Himself. Jesus stated the Spirit bore witness to Him, and He bore witness to the Father, yet He and the Father are one and the same. Deuteronomy 17 informs us that a person can be put to death only with at least two witnesses, and remember there were two witnesses at the death of Christ.

Three represents perfection (Luke 13:32); one plus one, plus one, equals three, Father, Son, and Holy Spirit. "Holy, holy, holy" is sung before the throne of God in Revelation 4 and Isaiah 6; it is referring to the "perfect holiness" at the throne of God. Another way to look at it would be one plus two equaling three, "God confirmed as perfect."

Four represents judgment or warning (Isaiah 51, Revelation). One plus three equals four,-"God's perfect judgment", or three plus one equals four, the "perfect God of judgment." Two plus two equals four; "God testifies to Himself and confirms He equals judgment."

Five represents the signs from God to help man see. Three plus two equals five, "perfect confirmation as a sign from God," and one plus four equals five, a "God of judgment who warns us with signs."

Six represents man, freedom, imperfection or the pride of man (Jeremiah 34). Three times two equals six, "a perfect confirmation to man," while two plus four equals six, "confirmed judgment on man." Six also represents liberty and freedom for all (Genesis 2, Jeremiah 34, and Revelation). Think how this relates so far to the number of the antichrist, the number of man, 666. You could define this in three ways: 1) man's perfect pride in man, 2) the perfection of rights for man's freedom, or 3) man's perfect system for mankind.

When God uses a set of three numbers being the same, it is another representation of perfection. For instance the number, one thousand, (1,000) with three zeros. When we multiply numbers by ten, "holiness," we see a definition of that number. This also works with 100, the two zeros representing "confirmation." The three zeros in 1,000 indicate "perfection"; in Judges 15, we see Samson supporting this conclusion. Samson put torches on the tails of three hundred foxes to set fire to the Philistines' fields. Later, three thousand men come to take him prisoner. When in the presence of the Philistines, the ropes fall off, and Samson killed a thousand men with a jawbone of a donkey. In the context of this event, God's holiness was perfectly stacked with holiness through Samson's actions. If you broke the number down, it might be something like this: one times ten, times ten, times ten equals a thousand. God is "one," then we have a set of three tens to represent "perfect holiness"; God's "perfect holiness" is thus demonstrated in Samson's killing of the Philistines; the cards were stacked in Samson's favor. Regarding the three hundred foxes; Again God's "perfect holiness confirmed" thru the act of Samson through judgment upon the Philistines by God.

The number 666 is a counterfeit number of God, but what is the true number this one counterfeits? In order to be a counterfeit number there must be a true number, right? Here is a little exercise using a set of three numbers within the basic number system of ten. Notice seven sets describe the person of God stand out. Two sets bear witness to God, and one counterfeit set of the antichrist is in the numbers one through ten. Take the first set of the number one in a set of three, or 111, meaning, "He is the perfect God," The only God, there is no other.

Number 222 would be defined as "the perfect witness, a description of Jesus, the perfect witness to the Father". Take 333; "God is perfectly perfect," and this needs no explanation.

In 444, God is the "perfect judge." The number 555 is defined as Jesus (God), a "perfect sign to man" or "a perfect sign from God". Skip 666 and consider 777 as "God of perfect completion and purity." The next two numbers 8 and 9, bear witness to God. We could define 888 as "God perfectly set apart from other gods." How about 999? He is "a God perfectly preparing the world for perfect holiness," which is a set of three tens'. I am not aware of any Scripture that defines God in this manner, but it does seem to work; it compares and identifies the counterfeit, the antichrist, to the true Christ. The true God defined above compared to the counterfeit god, 666, or the "perfect system (god) of man." It somehow seems to work. Why else would God identify the antichrist by a number? Again, within the numbers of one thru ten, seven of the sets of three numbers define God, two bear witness to God, and one identifies the counterfeit.

This observation helps us understand that the "numbers" in the Bible do indeed have reasons. We can also see a pattern in using sets of two numbers, which we will get into in a bit. For now, continue looking at the individual numbers within numbers. Remember that numbers can be added or multiplied as well as viewed individually in the Scriptures; again, the context defines the definition.

Seven represents completion, purification, purity, cleansing, or time of rest or reflection (Exodus, Numbers 19, and Leviticus 8). There are several ways to break seven down. Two plus five means "a confirmed sign that equals completion"; three plus four indicates "perfect judgment equals completion, or purification;" six plus one indicates, "Man is designed to be with God to be complete." Three plus three plus one "indicating two perfect witnesses for God, that equals completion and purity." If you use this in reference to the Son and the Holy Spirit, it works, just as it does when the two thieves witnessed Jesus' death. One witness unto heaven, and the other unto eternity apart from God. How about the sum of the two witnesses during the tribulation, that are each dead for three and one half days (two times three and a half) equals seven. We must recognize the warning from the two witnesses as representing a time of cleansing and purification, in the latter days before being resurrected by God.

Eight represents set apart, selected, chosen. The Bible contains limited references to eight. However, there are important insights to the use of numbers within numbers here. God saved eight people in the ark when He destroyed the world by water; this could be broken down as two times four equals eight, recognized as a "confirmed judgment upon the world," with Noah and his family being "set apart from the world." Noah was recognized in Scriptures as one person with seven others; Take seven plus one to represent "purification by God," which equaled the eight being "set apart or selected by God" to be saved from judgment upon the world (Deuteronomy 4).

God also required the male children to be circumcised on the eighth day after seven days of purification. If you take three (perfection) plus five, (a sign) to equal eight and break it down with the definitions above, you have circumcision being "a perfect sign of the Jews being set apart, chosen." A sign that separates the Jews from any other people, chosen and selected by God. Two times four equals "confirmed judgment on those that have been set apart." Remember that Scriptures state that God's judgment begins with the house of God. Take two plus six equals seven plus one, "confirmation that the Jews were to separate themselves from the world, in order to be complete in God."

Nine is used most frequently to designate time periods for preparation for holiness. It is used frequently in prophecy and is definitely symbolic. According to the law given by Moses. The evening of the ninth day was to be a time of preparing for the tenth day of holiness, the Day of Atonement; it was to be much like the Sabbath (Leviticus 23).

Eight plus one indicates, "Set apart for God for preparation". What if we reverse the order of the formula with nine equaling two times four plus one? This could be defined as "preparation for a confirmed judgment by God." Six plus three equates to "man's perfection or perfect man for a period of time before the coming of holiness." Five plus four is a "sign of judgment before holiness." Remember earlier in using a set of the number three, here is a set used differently: three, plus three, plus three, "to be in perfect perfection, before attaining holiness." Seven plus two broken down would mean, "Completion confirmed." We can also reverse the formula and come up with "confirmed completion to prepare for holiness." Think of this in context of the ninth hour in which Jesus died. Do you think this too could be accidental or by coincidence?

Ten represents God's holiness, His power, His righteousness, and the law of God. It is interesting to note that the sum of the two most important, most used, and most significant of numbers, three and seven, is ten. If you combine God's three entities, Father, Son and Holy Spirit, with His seven spirits, you get ten, "God's holiness, His power, His purity, and His complete and perfect righteousness." This is a perfect example of numbers within numbers. We have already learned that three is "perfect" and seven is "complete" and pure. The seven spirits of the Lord are defined as, 1) the Spirit of the Lord, 2) Spirit of wisdom, 3) Spirit of understanding, 4) the Spirit of counsel, 5) Spirit of might, 6) Spirit of knowledge, and 7) the Spirit of the fear of the Lord (Isaiah 11). These are also seen at the throne of God in Revelation. I believe the Holy Spirit is the sum of the seven spirits of God. This is another example of numbers in numbers and discovering the God of creation and the God of order. I find this to be fascinating, that three "perfect," plus seven "complete and pure" equals ten, the holiness of God or the "perfect, complete, and pure God of Holiness." Ten can also be understood to mean "righteous law."

God chose Israel to be an example in seven ways in Deuteronomy 4. These again are, by trials, by signs, by wonders, by war, by a mighty hand, by an outstretched arm, and by terrors. Deuteronomy 26 specifies that Israel be chosen in an additional three ways: for praise, for a name, and for honor.

This is a case of numbers within numbers by using two specific numbers to represent why God chose Israel; three symbolizes to be made perfect, and seven represents completion; together, they equal ten; "the Israelites were perfectly chosen to be a complete and holy people unto the Lord." In Deuteronomy 4, we learn that "Israel was chosen to be looked upon as an example of a great nation with wise and understanding people."

Any number in the Bible multiplied by ten signifies "holiness, by the law or with righteousness." One hundred is understood to be ten times ten, or "confirmed holiness;" It can also be broken down as one, times ten, times ten or "God's holiness confirmed or witnessed to"; three hundred- three times ten, times ten, is "perfect, confirmed holiness." In Judges 7, Gideon prepared 32,000 men for battle. They were to fight the army of the Midianites that were too many to number. The Lord told Gideon to reduce the number by a process of elimination. The amount was lowered to 300, who ended up defeating the Midianites with God as their defender. This clearly demonstrated the number of men to go to war was to give God the glory for the victory of the battle. So why three hundred? It was to be recognized the defeat of the Midianites was to reflect the glory to God. Three times ten, times ten, in this passage demonstrates His "perfect and confirmed glory, honor and power."

Take the Ten Commandments; "the law for holiness." The laws of God are summed up in ten laws. Ten is used repeatedly throughout Scripture as a factor of multiplication, but you will also see ten added to a number; ten plus one equates to the "holiness of God." If we define three plus seven as "perfect, complete holiness," we can put that in the context of the crucifixion; Christ was buried for three days during the seven days of Passover. Six plus four is "man's judgment by holiness," two plus eight means "confirmed to be set apart, unto holiness." Two times five is a "confirmed sign of holiness." The Ten Commandments were confirmed by being written twice. Ten, times one, plus ten times one, or the "confirmed law of God."

In Deuteronomy 6, Moses told the people to bind the sign of the law on their hands. Note we have two hands with five fingers each, equaling ten; even our hands are designed to remind us of the laws of God. Every time we go about our day, our hands are to remind us of God's ten laws and check our behavior to see if we are in line with Gods holiness. This would make a great sermon. God's design is by no accident. This merely shows that it does not matter how the numbers are broken down, it still somehow works. By the way, remember Goliath? He had six toes on each foot and six fingers on each hand. He was the biological result of demons having sex with people. He stood over nine feet tall. The symbolism is in the number six, do you see it? With six fingers on each hand, twelve fingers in all, being of tall statue (three cubits), and a by product of demons. Goliath "was the perfect man with authority" according to Satan. He was killed by one small stone by a young boy that represented God.

Eleven -Occasionally you find an odd number like the number eleven found in Exodus 26. Here we see God specifying eleven curtains. They were to be made of goat hair to be put over the temple to cover the Ark of the Covenant on the outside of the Tent of Meeting. Five were to be on one side and six on the other side. This seemed odd to me until I broke it down using the formula and put it in context, that being; five representing "a sign," and six representing "for man," with the sum being ten plus one, "the holiness of God." When the Jews looked at the tabernacle from the outside, they were always being reminded of God's covering over them and His covering over the Ark of the Covenant. The coverings were meant to be "a sign to man, of God's holy covering over them, a sign they had been chosen to holiness by God." Remember also that goats were designated and sacrificed as sin offerings; this too was symbolic.

What happens if we break down eleven in a different format or formula? Taking five times two, plus one equals, "a sign confirmed from God" that equals ten plus one, "the holiness of God." Inside the tabernacle was the Ark of the Covenant containing the Ten Commandments. Let us take four being symbolic of "judgment" by the law, and seven, "completion"; this put together is "judgment being completed by the God of holiness," or one plus ten. How about eight, plus three, equals ten plus one? This represents the Jews being "set apart with perfection to reveal the holiness of God."

One can conclude that no matter how you look at eleven in Exodus, it was a sign to man of God's holiness and covering over Israel. Could this all be by accident, or was this all symbolic of a message from God? You have to admit it is a bit odd, but let's continue.

Section Thirteen

The Number Twelve

Twelve represents "authority of God." In the Scriptures, we see the selection by God of twelve disciples and twelve tribes of Israel. Let's take the obvious first: two plus ten equals twelve; "confirmed holiness equals authority." Other ways to break the number down include adding seven plus five, "a complete sign of authority." How about, two times six equals twelve, or "a confirmation to man with Gods authority." Three times four means "perfect judgment that equals authority." We see a demonstration of this in Revelation's description of the gates of the New Jerusalem: the twelve gates with three angels at each describe "perfect authority." Eight plus four refers to those that are "set apart for judgment by authority."

It is interesting to note the two sets of twelve elders sitting with God that pronounce judgment on man in Revelation. These twenty-four elders consist of twelve leaders coming from the twelve tribes of Israel and the twelve disciples. Ishmael also had twelve sons, which are recognized today as Muslims; this by the way is the lineage of the antichrist, the counterfeit. The lineage God recognizes as true, is that from the twelve tribes of Israel or Jacob.

When Jesus fed five thousand men plus women and children, He started with five loaves of bread and two fish with twelve baskets of food left over. Let's look at 5,000 first; The first observation is the obvious numbers; a set of three zeros being understood as (perfect), then number five (sign to man). Another way to look at this is five times ten, times ten, times ten; This miracle, which happened at the beginning of Jesus' ministry, was a "sign to man of the perfect holiness of Jesus." Then take the five loaves and two fish, which equal seven, "a confirmed sign of purity or completion." Put it all together and you get this: Jesus performed a miracle that demonstrated "a perfect sign to man, a confirmed sign, of His complete authority." We reach this conclusion by first recognizing the 5,000. Then five loaves of bread and two fish added together that equal seven, with a remainder of twelve. Jesus later commissioned the twelve disciples and gave them authority over demons and sickness.

We also see a prophecy in Zephaniah in reference to the latter days in which Israel is attacked at twelve noon; In this case we break the number twelve down in several ways to understand the message. This is to symbolize God's act of confirmed holiness (two plus ten), a sign of purification (five plus seven), and perfect judgment (three times four) upon Israel for their sin. It is a sign indicating that God is the authority behind the events to come upon Israel.

In Exodus 28, we see the design of the breastplate of Aaron, the head priest; it had three sets of four stones. We are told the twelve stones represented the judgment on Israel. Broken down it would look like this; three times four equals "perfect judgment with complete authority."

Number Twelve References

Twelve tribes of Israel (Genesis 15).

Twelve tribes of Ishmael (Genesis 17).

Abraham's brother had twelve children (Genesis 22).

Jacob had twelve sons (Genesis 30).

Moses asked Pharaoh twelve times to let the Israelites go (Exodus 5–11).

The Lord of the Jews supplied twelve wells of water on the third day. This is at the beginning of their fleeing from Egypt and the start of forty years in the wilderness (Exodus 15).

Twelve pillars were built at the bottom of Mount Sinai after the Ten Commandments were given (Exodus 24).

Twelve stones adorned Aaron's breastplate (Exodus 28).

On the dedication of the Tent of Meeting, there were twelve center plates, twelve golden plates, twelve golden basins and twelve silver basins. Also twelve bulls, twelve rams and twelve goats were offered as a sin offering. Note the four objects of twelve, and the set of three types of animals necessary for the sin offering, seven sets of twelve (Numbers 7).

Moses picked twelve men to be spies (Numbers 13).

God gave twelve curses upon the people for their disobedience (Deuteronomy 27).

Twelve stones were placed as a memorial honoring God performing the miracle when the Nile River separated and dried up, allowing the twelve tribes of Israel to pass over to the other side (Joshua 4).

Twelve men of Ishbosheth and twelve men of David fought it out to death (2 Samuel 2).

King Solomon had twelve officers over Israel (1 Kings 4).

Elijah builds an altar with twelve stones, and three times pours four (3x4) big jars of water upon the altar to where it filled the trench around the altar. Elijah then prays that the authority of God would be demonstrated to the people. God strikes the altar with fire and consumes the sacrifice and the water. Here we have two sets of twelve to confirm God's authority. We also have three times four, "perfect in judgment" or three plus four equaling seven, "complete." Put this all together you have "A God that is complete with perfect judgment that demonstrated or confirmed His authority" (I Kings 18).

David had twelve sons (1 Chronicles 14).

Twelve months after Daniel interpreted his dream, Nebuchadnezzar was turned into a beast due to his pride (Daniel 4).

Twelve sins are spoken of against Israel (Hosea 4).

Israel in the latter days will be attacked at twelve noon (Zephaniah 1–3).

Jesus picked twelve disciples (Matthew 10, Luke 5–6).

Jesus feeds five thousand men with twelve baskets left over (Matt. 14, John 6).

Jesus sent the twelve to teach and perform miracles (Mark 6).

Jesus was twelve years old when his parents accidently left Him in the city for three days (Luke 2).

Jesus gave authority to the twelve disciples over demons and sickness (Luke 9).

The disciples are given authority to judge the twelve tribes of Israel. (Matthew 19, Luke 22).

Four angels at the four corners of earth are seen next holding back all the winds. Another angel appears from the "rising of the sun" and he calls out to the angels to hold back from destroying the earth until all of the servants of God are sealed upon their forehead. That number is twelve thousand out of each of the twelve tribes of Israel (Revelation 7).

A great woman appears in Revelations who has twelve crowns on her head (Revelation 12).

One of seven angels comes to John and shows him the New Jerusalem with a great wall around it. There are three gates facing four directions, with three angels at each gate. We have twelve gates and four sets of nine angels facing each direction with thirty-six angels in all. The twelve gates are made of pearls. Each gate has the name of the twelve tribes of Israel. There are twelve foundations with twelve precious stones with the names of the twelve apostles. The Tree of Life is there and bears twelve kinds of fruit (Revelation 21–22).

NOTES

Section Fourteen

The Number Thirty

Thirty represents "perfect holiness" or "perfect righteousness." Now we start to see the significance of understanding the basic numbers and how they "stack" or build upon each other. Remember they all start with the number one. Thirty can be broken down in several ways. The first with three, (perfection) times' ten, (holy) equals "perfect holiness." Jesus was thirty when He began His ministry, which incidentally was for three years. One formula could be specified as five times six equals a "sign to man that equals perfect holiness (three times ten)," referring to Jesus in this case. Jesus was sold out because of His "perfect holiness" by Judas for thirty pieces of silver. If we took three times five, times two, and broke it down, it would mean a "perfect sign confirmed," that equals "the perfect will of God, His perfect holy plan," fulfilling the prophecy of Isaiah. Another way we can break down the numbers in the passage where Christ is betrayed, could be seven times four, plus two, "complete judgment" by the Pharisees "confirmed" that would result "with perfect holiness." This is an example of what Satan meant for evil, God changed for good.

Here is a theory that, though I cannot prove it, is interesting. It is based on the realization that numbers are important to God and there is reason in His numbers. In order to understand this you must realize that a day to the Jews starts at sunset and ends at sunset the next day; Jesus was crucified around 3:00 in the afternoon on the sixth day of Passover and died around 9:00 that evening. About an hour or so later, possibly ninety minutes, "in preparation for holiness" it became the beginning of the seventh day of Passover, known as the Sabbath. Jesus during this hour plus period before the Sabbath, was buried in a tomb close by before the sunset. This is to be noted as the first day. We also know He was in the tomb for one full day of twenty-four hours, until about 10:30 p.m. at the end of the Sabbath. This was considered the second day of being in the tomb. He had been dead for about twenty-five hours at that point; this is assuming His third day in the tomb began after 10:00 p.m.: We will assume it was until 10:33 p.m. It is recorded that he rose from the dead early in the morning on the third day. Based upon numbers my thought is this. From 10:33 p.m. on the Sabbath until He arose, had to be no more than probably seven hours. I think He rose on the third day at 3:33 in the morning, the "perfect resurrection." Remember in chapter three the number 333 meant "a perfect God, with a perfect plan, and a perfect ending." He had lain in the tomb from 10:33 P.M. to 3:33 A.M., an additional five hours for a total of thirty hours, again with thirty representing "perfect holiness."

The five hours on the third day was to be a sign. To me this just makes sense. Another possibility is that He arose at 3:37 P.M., which would be understood as "perfection confirmed completely," or "His perfectness is confirmed and complete." How would you interpret that possibility? This is mentioned only to stimulate thought, to challenge one's thinking about the significance and the importance of numbers to God. He arose at a specific time to symbolize His perfection and to complete what He came for; we don't have that recorded for us, but there is enough evidence based on numbers that there was a specific time in the resurrection of Christ. It is without a doubt; Jesus did not rise from the grave at some random hour of time.

It is interesting to note the similarities in what I am writing about, and Judaism. In Judaism thirty represents "perfection of divine order," the product of three times ten. Three represents "holiness or fulfillment" and ten represents "absolute completeness." If indeed Jesus was in the grave for thirty hours it would mean that, His resurrection was "a sign of the fulfillment and completeness of a perfect plan by divine order." More on the numbers in Judaism later.

Number Thirty References

The reward for answering Sampson's riddle was two sets of thirty garments (Judges 14).
David was thirty years old when he began to reign (2 Samuel 5).
Jesus was betrayed for thirty pieces of silver (Zechariah 11, Matthew 26).
Jesus began His ministry at age thirty (Luke 3).
There will be thirty minutes of silence in heaven when the seventh seal is broken (Revelation 8).

Interesting Notes on Thirty

Joseph was thirty when his service for Pharaoh began.
Israel wept at the death of Aaron for thirty days.
Daniel was commanded to worship Nebuchadnezzar for thirty days.

Section Fifteen

The Number Forty

Forty is "judgment by holiness, or a time of testing for holiness," the product of four times ten. Do you think it was coincidental that Noah was in the ark for forty days and nights? That Moses was forty years old when he murdered the Egyptian. That forty years later, he was chosen to lead God's people out of Egypt. That he received the Ten Commandments after forty days and nights on Mount Sinai? That he fasted and prayed an additional forty days and nights for the people of Israel not to be destroyed by Gods anger? That another forty days and nights were required to rewrite the Commandments for the second time and receive instructions for the building of the temple? That the Israelites were in the desert for forty years? That Moses sent spies to Canaan for forty days? That Samson mocked Israel for forty days before he was killed by David?

Do you think it coincidental that Elijah was fed by the Ravens sustaining him for forty days. That David and Solomon reigned for forty years? That Jesus was tempted after forty days of fasting and remained on earth for forty days after His resurrection? Or that forty angels, according to Revelation, will deliver God's wrath on mankind? Do you think all this is by chance? Could man have planned this? Or is God indeed a God of order, who sends messages within messages to us?

Forty represents a time of testing, proving, judgment, or building humbleness. It is a case of numbers within numbers that can have different meanings and yet interchangeable. We have the same thing happen in the English language. The word *point* is an example; it means to prove, case in point, it refers to the tip of a spear or arrow, and it can indicate direction, say, if we are pointing somewhere or at someone. It can refer to the stock market, a loan, or an intersection of two lines. In fact, there are almost a hundred definitions for the word. I hope that this makes my "point." Sometimes in Scriptures, there are different meanings to numbers but their definitions become clearer as they intertwine with the particular scriptures in reference. If we took the obvious break down of four (judgment) times ten (holiness) it would mean, Jesus "the judge by holiness, His judgment is by the law, or judgment by God," Understanding that forty is the product of numbers multiplied or added together.

Forty can be a reference to punishment; referring to when one received forty lashes. It can also be understood as three times ten, plus ten or "perfect holiness confirmed." The product of three times ten, plus ten determines this. By using two tens implies a confirmation. An example would be after Jesus fasted for forty days "confirming His perfect holiness."

In Judaism, forty is a product of either four times ten or five times eight, both symbolizing trials and testing. Jews believe four represents the fulfillment of God's plan and ten represents absolute completeness. Eight for them is symbolic of a new beginning.

Number Forty References

It rained upon the earth in judgment for forty days and forty nights with Noah (Genesis 7).

It took forty days to embalm Jacob (Genesis 50).

Moses was forty when he killed the Egyptian (Exodus 2, Acts 7), and forty years later, God chose him to lead the Israelites out of bondage (Exodus 6, Acts 7), which took forty years. Note the three sets of forty.

The Israelites ate manna for forty years so that they would be humbled (Exodus 16).

Moses received the Ten Commandments after forty days and nights on Mount Sinai the first time (Exodus 24).

Moses returned to Mount Sinai for forty days and nights to receive the Ten Commandments the second time (Exodus 34).

Moses sent spies to Canaan for forty days (Numbers 13).

Because of the Israelites' complaining, they were punished for forty years and did not receive the promise (Numbers 14).

It was necessary that the Israelites were in the wilderness for forty years for testing and to build their sense of humility (Deuteronomy 8).

Moses for forty days and nights intercedes for the Israelites, that God would have mercy on them (Deuteronomy 9).

Moses fasted three times that God would have mercy on the Israelites for their disobedience while in the wilderness for forty years. Each time was for a period of forty days and nights (Deuteronomy 9, Acts 7).

Forty stripes were designated as punishment for wrongdoing (Deuteronomy 25).

Caleb was forty when instructed to spy for Moses (Joshua 24).

Many rulers reigned for forty years (Judges).

God gave Israel over to the Philistines for forty years (Judges 40).

Goliath challenged the Israelites for forty days before being killed by David (1 Samuel 17).

David and Solomon each reigned for forty years (1 Kings 2, 1 Kings 11).

Ravens feed Elijah, which sustains him for forty days; Jehoash also reigned for forty years (1 Kings 19).

Nehemiah reminds Israel that during their forty years in the desert, their clothes never wore out and God always provided food and water. In the daytime, they were led by a pillar of smoke, and at night by a pillar of fire (Nehemiah 9).

Solomon was king for forty years (2 Chronicles 9).

The Lord punished and admits His anger on the Israelites for forty years because of their disobedience (Psalm 95).

Ezekiel lay on his side for forty days as a prophetic statement for Judah (Ezekiel 4).

Jonah preaches to the people of Nineveh for forty days, about the judgment of God unless they repent. The people turn back to God (Jonah 3).

Jesus was led into the wilderness to fast for forty days for the purpose of being tempted (Matthew 3–4, Luke 4).

Jesus remained on earth for forty days after His resurrection, proving His holiness (Acts 1).

Paul received forty stripes five times (2 Corinthians 14).

There are a total of forty angels that deliver the wrath and judgment from God upon the world in the end (Revelation).

Interesting notes on forty

Moses was forty when he killed the Egyptian; he was called to lead the Israelites out of Egypt forty years later, and he spent forty years in the wilderness. The Israelites were in the desert for forty years to learn humility. There are three sets of forty in Moses' life: The first set being he was forty when he killed the Egyptian, forty years went by before he was called by God to lead the Israelites out of Egypt, and he spent forty years in the desert leading the people. The second set was the three events of forty days each involved in receiving of the law. The third set of forty is when he prayed and fasted forty days and nights, three times for God not to destroy His people during the forty years while leading Israel (Acts 7).

NOTES

Section Sixteen

The Number Fifty

Fifty is usually a number used for measurement, "a sum equaling the whole" such as five times ten, a sign to man of holiness or righteousness. It is used as a specification of measurement in the building of the Ark, and the Temple of God. Noah, Moses, and David received specific measurements involving fifty. The temple had many requirements that consisted of fifty; this refers to both the original temple built by Solomon and the New Temple upon the return of Christ.

The obvious break down would be five times ten to be understood as "a sign of holiness." It is often used in determining the quantity of cubits or in reference to a quantity of people used in multiples of fifty. If you were to break down the number five hundred as five times ten, times ten, with ten used twice, and remember that two of the same number refers to a confirmation: Interpretation- "a sign of holiness confirmed, or holiness stacked on holiness."

How about the five thousand men fed by Jesus with only two fish and five loaves of bread, with twelve baskets remaining. In this case, we don't add or multiply the numbers we just recognize the numbers and their meanings. First, we have 5,000 men; a five followed by three zeros would be "a sign of perfection." Then seven to be broken down as two plus five, "a confirmed sign." Next taking the twelve baskets left over to represent "authority." Then put it into context, adding the message not the numbers together you get that this miracle was "a confirmed sign to mankind, witnessing a perfect sign of authority, Jesus." The bread would also be symbolic that Jesus was the bread of life. This whole event was to be understood that Jesus was under the authority of God himself and no other. Another possible understanding of 5,000 could be five times ten, times ten, times ten. This meant, "Jesus was a sign of perfect holiness."

Three sets of fifty men were sent to kill Elijah in the first chapter of 2 Kings. God sent fire upon the first two sets and destroyed them. This demonstrated to man Elijah's righteousness; he was to be recognized as "a sign of righteousness or holiness." According to the Torah, there were fifty days from the day of Passover when Israel fled from Egypt to the day that Moses received the Ten Commandments on Mount Sinai. Jewish tradition recognizes number fifty as one times ten plus forty; meaning the "God of holiness will be the judge of holiness."

Here is a very uncomfortable possibility regarding Babylon, the last empire of man. It is a nation, that has by its trade and marketing influence has polluted the world. It is a country surrounded by and contains many waters. It is a nation represented by a great eagle (Bald eagle) and a lady of freedom (statue of liberty). It is a country that has supported Israel with military power in the latter days, later, to only in the end, betray them. It is a country of many languages and cultures, and promotes homosexuality. It is a country that promotes self-indulgence, and is rich with materialism; it is a nation full of pride and coveting. All these references to this last "Babylon" describe a country in the last days.

What if this empire of the last days comprises of fifty states? This empire will be devastated by a huge earthquake that actually splits the nation into four parts. This is yet to come. I think by now you realize what country I am referring to. After all, the United States will not be around at the end of the tribulation. Also, note that this nation will have a change of heart and attack Israel after helping it for almost seventy years. A couple of these events are yet to happen. I know I am sticking my neck out here, and many will come against what I say, but I believe this to be one reason for this writing.

Babylon being split up into four parts is literal and symbolic of what will happen to Babylon, that is "judgment." So now we have a nation composed of fifty states split into four areas. Fifty states could be understood as five times ten, times one; Interpretation; "Babylon will be judged as a sign to the world by the holiness of God."

Number Fifty References

Genesis 6; Exodus 26, 27, 36; 1 Kings 7; Ezekiel 40, 48.

References about Babylon (KJV)

Isaiah 13, 47, 59; Daniel 2; Jeremiah 50, 51; Habakkuk 1; Revelation 18.

Section Seventeen

The Number Seventy

Seventy represents complete holiness, complete purification by or for holiness. It is the product of seven times ten. In the Hebrew Bible, the Torah, the two numbers thirty and forty are recognized as very important. When one turns thirty years old, it is "the age when one reaches the prime of our energy and royalty is attained." Forty represents "a change or transition, indicating the concept of renewal, a new beginning." The Torah also refers to forty in reference to "The four sides of the world, each containing ten powers."

Forty lashes were meant to change criminals' behaviors. When one was to be beaten with forty lashes, it was meant to bring the offender to the law and to point out a change, a transition and atonement for their wrongdoing, "judgment by holiness." Seventy to the Jew represents "perfection of a divine order." In Judaism, seventy is understood as the "sum that makes the whole," or "the sum of the parts." It is attained by the sum of three times ten and four times ten. Compare this to the definitions of the number thirty and forty spoken of earlier where thirty represents "perfect holiness" and forty represents "holy judgment." The sum of the two equaling "perfect holiness with or by holy judgment."

Seventy can be broken down several ways. Three plus four, times ten yields "a perfect judgment by His righteousness which equals complete holiness." Compare this to the Hebrew definition being "perfection by divine order."

According to Jewish teaching, the number seventy represents the sum of the parts; this is referring to the many ways to break the sum down, yet the sum or the product meaning the same. One way it can be broken down is by the product of seven (meaning divine completion) times ten, (absolute completeness). Seven times ten refers to the full range of components to achieve wholeness. They believe that wholeness is achieved within a person when one attains the seventy forces of illumination within man, the so-called seventy faces of the Torah. They believe they will be the one nation against seventy other nations in the end times, the nation that unites the world to worship the one true God. They believe they are the path to the nations being unified into wholeness, determining the world's destiny. The last seventy years referred to by Jeremiah, they consider as "seventy cycles;" they also believe there are seventy impure forces enraged against Israel.

The Jewish people claim that they exist for the sole purpose of integrating the seventy forces of the world toward the one God. Their purpose is to incorporate the seventy forces of man toward one single goal, "To love the Lord your God with all of your heart, all of your soul and all your resources." Israel will unite the seventy nations, fulfilling the seventy facets of the Torah, proclaiming the oneness of God in the Messianic era; "On that day, God will be One and His name One" (Zechariah 14).

All of these definitions make the whole, thus the Jewish saying goes "the whole will be greater than the sum of its parts." The final endpoint of creation being when Israel, while observing the Torah will return to Jerusalem, the city of holiness in worship of their God." Jews claim that there are seventy names for the Torah and that there are seventy names for Jerusalem. When all these parts come together in wholeness, that will be what establishes a unified state. Seventy is the sum of all the holy days they celebrate in one year. They believe there are seventy angels ruling over the Jewish nation. Seventy is the number seven magnified by ten, achieving the full range of components. Compare the Jewish definitions and the definitions in this writing; can you see the similarity?

God is a God of order and the God of all creation. The numbers He uses are not accidents; they are divine planning. God uses numbers to symbolically reveal the significance of His messages. In Scriptures, we get to see a few of these revealed and some of the insights given to us by God. Consider this thought; the facts within God's Word have limited meaning unless we understand the significance of the facts. A simple example would be having knowledge of the death and resurrection of Christ without understanding the significance personally. We must know why He paid the price for our sin by His death and the importance of His resurrection. The fact that He rose from the dead on the third day, why? What is the significance? As Jesus said, it was so He would be "perfected," that is significant.

Seventy men died because they looked inside the Ark of the Covenant. Why seventy? I believe it was to demonstrate the "complete holiness," that man was not qualified to look upon. Remember when God called Jacob into Egypt and declared he and sixty-nine others were to be the beginning of a nation, seventy people, and the start of the Jewish nation. Three days after the Israelites were in the heat of the desert, the Lord provided seventy palm trees for a place of rest for them, it was also meant to be a sign, to them. Again, let us break the number seven and the number ten down in several ways. First note God provided the shade after the third or "perfect" day, revealing His perfect timing of demonstrating His perfect care for Israel.

Next let's look at the different possible breakdowns for the number seventy: two plus five, times ten is a "confirmed sign of holiness and His power," three plus four, times ten is "perfect judgment by holiness," six plus one, times ten is "man with God equals holiness," and two times three, plus one, times ten, is "a confirmation by a perfect God of holiness." Any of these combinations work in reference to the act of providing seventy trees of shade as rest for Israel.

A passage that is often overlooked is in Exodus 24 revealing a period just before Moses received the Ten Commandments; seventy elders went with Moses and Aaron to Mount Sinai and ate in the presence of the Lord before Joshua and Moses ascended to the top of the mountain to receive the Commandments.

My study of numbers led me to study prophecy and helped clarify questions pertaining to the latter days. The book of Revelation is a great example of the importance of numbers in the end. I hope this study has been a great insight into God's design and plan for His creation and the end, the alpha and the omega. Nothing in His creation is without purpose and reason, even mathematics. Consider the symbolism in and within numbers and see if it makes sense in context. I am sure you will discover more than I have listed in the use of numbers. One thing is for certain: In today's world, man wants God to conform to man. It is a condition of the sinful nature of man. God designed us to conform to Him, we have reversed His law. Because of this, God's wrath must come upon all flesh.

An example of this, recently Pope Francis was quoted as saying he wants to preach the joy of the gospel, not the truth of the gospel. This comment was in response to him being questioned about the acceptance of same sex marriages. I think what he is saying is that he wants to teach what tickles the ears, not what challenges the heart.

I hope this has given you insight regarding seventy. Now here is where I stick my neck out, one of the main purposes of this writing. The number seventy in Daniel is probably the most controversial and most important number in reference to the last days. The prophets Jeremiah, Zechariah, and Daniel prophesied the coming of the Messiah at the end of seventy years once Israel became a nation again. We just discovered that seven times ten is interpreted as "complete holiness, holiness completed, purification, cleansing with or by Holiness." Israel is to be under the authority or the wing of protection of Babylon for seventy years twice, and this happened once already.

We are told God will stretch His arm out once again against Israel; this is a warning that history will repeat itself, when Israel is again under Babylon's protection for seventy years in the fourth and last kingdom of the symbolic Babylon described and defined in Daniel 9.

This last seventy years designated by the prophets, refer to a final seven years within the seventy containing the wrath of God. These last seven years are described in Revelation. At the end of the last seven years, the Messiah will arrive to redeem Israel, at least what is left of it. Seventy breaks down to three (perfect) plus four (judgment) times ten (holiness) equals seventy; this is the symbolism of the seventy years, a "time of perfect judgment by holiness that will equal the complete (seven) holiness (ten times one) of God."

Daniel defined the seventy years to be sixty-two years plus seven years. I think this was declared and perhaps a bit misunderstood by Daniel as he was convinced that "seven" could not be shortened. I think he understood the total was not a complete set of seventy years. However, in a numbers-in-numbers sense, sixty-two represents six, "man's imperfection," times ten "of the law, the holiness of God," plus two, "confirmed". Add to this the final seven years, and it is short of seventy full years. Could this be symbolic of man being robbed of perfection? His falling short of holiness? This would support Scriptures that God declares that the end times have to be shortened or there would be no human left. Then symbolically an additional seven years showing God's cleansing and purification is completed in judgment.

If Daniel's prophecy was broken down as sixty-three and seven years, as stated by other prophets, this could be three, plus six times ten, plus seven equaling seventy. Translated as "perfect man against Holiness completed," that results in "perfect judgment by the holiness of God," or three plus four, times ten, times one. This is understood as the day of the Lord's wrath on mankind. Three (perfect), plus four (judgment), times' ten (holiness), times one equals a "perfect judgment to complete the holiness of God."

Zechariah prophesied that the last days would be sixty plus ten years. Jeremiah referred to the time Israel would be under Babylon as seventy years, at which time the Lord visits Israel. Daniel 9 also clarifies the number to be seventy years. It is understood later in other prophetic books that God will repeat that time of history on the Jews again. Either way, it is referred to as seventy years broken down into two separate periods that equal seventy or just short of seventy years.

This next section is going to be unpopular and will not be received well by many, but it is based on numbers and what we have learned so far. This next section will require an open mind, and I challenge all readers to maintain one, consider this, and watch for the signs. Sometimes we have all kinds of excuses to avoid facing what we do not like. I feel this next section contains the reason these discoveries about numbers were given to me, because it is time they were revealed. I believe we are in that seventy-year period that Jeremiah, Ezekiel, and Daniel spoke of referring to the last days.

Daniel clearly states that when Israel becomes a nation again, seventy years will determine the return of the Chosen One. This seems simple enough, however, there are several Hebrew calendars and they all differ from each other. This is due to the people of Israel being in captivity and separated from their country many times throughout their history. These calendars for the most part can vary by several years with another Hebrew calendar. Their calendars are based on lunar cycles, the stage of the ripening of local crops and holidays. The calendars are subject to change to keep their holidays on certain days of the year. It only makes sense that if God was making an example out of the Jews, He would use their calendar, not another. The question is which Hebrew calendar is correct?

The idea of Israel again becoming its own nation after thousands of years, was conceived on November 29, 1947, and it became a nation on May 18, 1948, a difference of about six months. This is according to the Chaldean calendar. With the Hebrew calendar both of those dates are in the year 5708 AM. This is because their calendar overlaps our calendar by about six months and every year this varies. On April 14, 2013, Israel celebrated its sixty-fifth year as a nation. What does this mean? How does it relate to seventy years? Remember in Daniel 9 and 10 the Messiah returns at the end of seventy years when Israel was thought to be a nation once again. This happened after some 2500 years in 1947-1948. Remember within that seventy years the last seven years were to be the great tribulation spoken of by the prophets. There are two possible explanations, the first: We are now in the first few years of the seven-year tribulation. This also would mean that Israel will be attacked most likely by the end of 2014 or 2015 by Iran, land of the Medes, and Syria spoken of in Daniel. This is a chilling, uncomfortable thought but a very good possibility. This would mean the return of the Lord could be as soon as the end of 2018 or 2019, give or take. The second possibility is that the seventy years is based on a calendar other than the most accepted AM Hebrew calendar. The AM refers to the most accepted Hebrew "calendar of the world." I guess there is a third explanation: I may be misinterpreting what the prophets claimed about the timing of the end.

Let's take 1948 as an interpretive reference point at which the events of the end begin. Since 1948, there have been several events that the Jews received more of the original promise land, the last was in 1967. This could alter the accuracy of interpretation of when the seventy years actually started in the eyes of God. However, if we use 1948 as a reference date and understand the Hebrew calendar is difficult to fully understand, then I will continue with this thought. The Hebrew AM calendar has thirteen months in a year and anywhere from 353 days to 385 days in a year; it is not based on seasons or a 365-day Chaldean year. Jews add and subtract days to make their specified holidays work.

In addition, the ancient Hebrew calendars over the years of captivity have been entwined with other cultures and changed several times. What makes the matter more confusing is that Jewish days are from sunset to sunset; Jews have more than four versions of calendars. However, I will use the most current and most commonly used, the AM calendar for my position. Incidentally, the "correct" calendar is also in accordance to which Rabbi you follow.

In this section, we will make a comparison of the Jewish calendar and our calendar for the last couple of years and a couple of years in the future. The day they celebrate being a nation once again is called Yom Ha'Atzmaut. Their 64th birthday as a nation was April 26, 2012. Their 65th birthday was celebrated on April 14 of 2013, their year 5773 AM. On May 5 of 2014, they celebrated their 66th year as a nation. They will celebrate their 67th year on April 22 of 2015. Their 68th year will be celebrated on May 11, 2016. On May 01, 2017, they will celebrate their 69th year. Their 70th year anniversary will be recognized on April 18, 2018. These dates are based on lunar cycles and are subject to change. These dates will be for the purpose of reference points only. Note that April 18, 2018 is on their third day of the second month of 5778. Remember the Lord visits Israel before the completion of the year 5778. What if He was to return some thirty or forty days before to complete His prophecies of being short of seventy years? His return would be in the year 5777. This is merely to point out the importance of seventy and how it relates to us today. We can all draw our own conclusions, but mine is this: somehow and in some way, we are in the latter days spoken of by the prophets. Understand we do not know the exact date, but we do have a proximity given to us by the prophets and by Jesus.

The year of 5777 could be interpreted as "a sign of perfect completion," what a way to end the world. The numbers five –"a sign," three sevens–"perfect," and seven representing "completion." Summed up as "a sign of perfect completion.".

This is a sign that trumps 666. A possibility? I will let you decide, but you have to admit it is more than interesting—it is just plain scary, and at the same time awesome! Consider this in prayer and fasting. Study the Word and watch for signs.

God's calendar is different from the many Jewish calendars and ours. It is interesting to note that Rabbi Aish was recently asked, "What would be the signs of the coming of the Messiah?" His response was that it would be a time of lost or decaying morals, values, and traditions. A time of lack of respect and of no correction (political correctness and injustice). It would be a time when religious studies would be despised, evil would twist the truth, and governments would become godless. There would also be a mass movement of Jews returning to Israel from around the world. My question is, how much more obvious do we need to get? If you are paying attention to the world current events, presently a mass Exodus of Jews from around the world are returning to their "homeland" of Israel. One cannot avoid admitting that all the other conditions mentioned by Rabbi Aish, are happening now.

Determining the exact date is difficult; even Jesus did not know the day or the hour. However, the prophets, including Jesus, defined a time, the season and approximately the year, when the wrath would come, to prepare us, so we are not caught by surprise.

If we take the literal translation of the seventy years referred to earlier by the prophets when Israel becomes a nation, and the fact that Israel just celebrated sixty-six years as a nation, this could mean only one thing: We are in the designated time now! We are in the first couple of years of the seven years of tribulation. Regardless of how it is calculated, it fits within 2018-2019 on our Chaldean calendar. A clue when the tribulation is in process is given to us; it will be when Israel is attacked by the land of the Medes (Iran) and Syria. Then being attacked by ancient Persia, which is most of the Middle Eastern countries. Later being attacked by their ally, Babylon (USA?). This all happens about the center of the tribulation.

As this is being written, we are at the doorsteps of Israel being attacked by Iran, the area of the ancient Medes, and Syria according to the prophets. This period we now live in fits in the prophecy of the Messiah coming seventy years after Israel became a nation again. We are now in the period of the last seven years within the seventy years before the complete wrath upon the world. Then Jesus will return, some will receive eternal life and some will receive eternal torment. The reader has to choose which one, no one else can do this for you.

Jesus referred to the fig tree, and to learn from the fig tree, in reference to the end of time. There is a symbolic message here also; the fig tree has always symbolized Israel. Perhaps this is a clue from Jesus so we will not be taken by surprise. Several references refer to a time of the year in which Israel is attacked. The fig tree is used as one of these references. Which incidentally there are two times a year in which the Fig tree bears fruit, once in the spring and once in the fall. It is written in that day "The fruit of the fig tree will be on the table."

There is one big hurdle that keeps many people from accepting this thinking; the temple is supposed to be built before the seven-year period starts. However, this is a misinterpretation. In Zechariah 6, we are told that at the **end** of the seven years of tribulation, Jesus himself will build the temple upon his return. This is after Israel and Jordon are destroyed in the last moments of the seven-year period. This is only one of many clues given to us about the last days. The temple has been built and destroyed twice already. It only makes since that Jesus would build the "perfect" (third) temple. The entire mountain where the temple will be located will be holy (Ezekiel 43).

Another hurdle is the rapture. If we are indeed in the tribulation, why has not the church been raptured? There are many Scriptures that refer to the saints in the end times being beheaded, some saints going to prison for ten days, and some making it through the tribulation, so I would not base my hopes on being raptured. For sure, there will be one at the end of the seven years in which believers meet Christ in the air. There also appears possibly to be a mid- partial rapture. The Lord refers in Revelation that he will keep His people in Babylon from that last hour. That last hour is in reference to just prior to Babylon being destroyed. I hope this will only give us a mentality to be ready by being in prayer and living lives worthy of praise to the Father. Also, that we are not confused and possibly losing our faith. We should have a mentality of desiring to witness to the lost, in hopes that some would be saved. Instead, we have received a mentality to run and escape from the mission God has called us to, the sharing of the "good news" when the world is falling apart. We are to be a witness, grounded in the faith, sharing His hope and truth with others, even during the time of testing. The church today tickles our ears with grace and the love of God. We forget that God is the same yesterday and today, that He is also a God of judgment as well.

When I began this study, I had no idea where it would go. If indeed, we are in the beginning stages one way or another of the latter days. Then it is true that time is short. The discovery of the symbolism of numbers has been revealed for a reason, that is, it is time to convince others, to warn people, and to declare that He is the God of love, revenge, and judgment. The message within this message on numbers is that we live a life of holiness and obedience. Be careful not to be deceived by exchanging truth for lies, regardless of the timing before His return.

Some may say this discovery on numbers is nothing but doom and gloom. My response to that is this. It depends on which side of the fence you are on. There are two sides of the fence, which side do you "testify to"? One side being focused on what you have in this world and lose it all, or the other side of the fence. That is, to lose everything in this world for him, and gain everything from Him. We must realize how blessed we are to witness the fulfillment of God's promises and to be willing to do what He asks of us. Understanding that we are chosen to tell others about Jesus and about eternal life, even in the midst of tribulation. We must realize that we have been selected for the greatest moment in history to be a witness to the "King of Kings and Lord of Lords" while on this earth. You must choose a "number" to follow. Which one do you choose? I have chosen, 3,7,10 for me, "perfect and complete holiness for me."

Number Seventy References

Abraham's father was seventy when Abraham was born (Genesis 11).
Seventy family members of Jacob moved to Egypt to begin the nation of Israel (Genesis 46). God began the nation of Israel with seventy and will end the nation with seventy (seventy years); Can you see the alpha and the omega message?
Seventy elders were with Moses before he ascended to the top of the mountain to receive the Commandments (Exodus 24).
Seventy elders are selected to help Moses with the burden of leading the Israelites. The Spirit of God came upon those seventy and they prophesied. It is also revealed in this passage what happened to the people for complaining about having only Manna to eat for forty years (Numbers 7).
Seventy men were destroyed for looking inside the ark of the covenant (1 Samuel 6).
Seventy palm trees were provided by God for shade to the Israelites after three days in the desert along with twelve wells of water (Exodus 15). The three days and the twelve wells of water represent the god who provided for them, the one with "perfect authority." The number seventy has been properly recorded in the King James Version and overlooked in other translations of the Bible. Note this is designated as numbers within numbers; it was designated

as "three score plus ten." Why was this not mentioned as just seventy palm trees? Look at the message within the numbers. A score equals two times ten. The equation for three score would be three times two, times ten, or "perfect confirmation for holiness." If we take three times two to equal six, then multiply by ten times one, we would have "perfect confirmation to man of the holiness from God." Then add ten, or holiness repeated, which equals seventy. What is the message for Israel within the numbers of the seventy trees? Let's put it together in a mathematical formula within the context. Three times two equals six, then take six times ten, plus ten, which equals seventy or seven times ten. The trees were a symbolic message of a "perfect confirmation of man's imperfect holiness, but with God, will equal God's complete holiness." Seventy trees could also represent in this case "complete shade (protection) or comfort, or rest for Israel was supplied by their God of holiness." The timing and the number of trees were a symbol to Israel of "a perfect confirmation from God demonstrating that Israel's holiness is dependent upon God's perfect and complete holiness."

Tyre is destroyed after playing the harlot for seventy years (Isaiah 21–23).

Jeremiah prophesied Israel would serve Babylon for seventy years, after which Babylon, the symbolic name for the last of the great nations will be destroyed; this is a case of history repeating itself. The Lord destroys the nation represented as the "last Babylon" by His Word. The Lord stretches his arm out against Israel twice. (Jeremiah 25)

At the end of seventy years, the Lord will return to Israel in the latter days (Jeremiah 29).

From the going forth of Israel to become a nation, it is seventy years to the desolation of Israel (Daniel 9).

Seventy years are designated to put an end to sin and an end to Jerusalem (Daniel 9). At the end of seventy years is "complete holiness," (seven times ten), when Jesus returns.

The angel that Zechariah saw asks the Lord, how much longer He will punish and refuse mercy on Israel? For His indignation has been upon Israel for three score and ten (70) years (Zechariah 1). This is to be formulated as three times two equals six, then taking the six, times ten, plus one times ten, meaning "perfect confirmation to (Israel) of man's lack of holiness, punished by God's holiness, equals complete holiness, (seven times ten)." This is in reference to the last days.

The fasting from the leadership of Israel for seventy years is for themselves (Zechariah 7).

We are told to forgive seven times seventy times (Matthew 18).

Jesus appointed seventy to preach and heal the sick (Luke 10).

Israel being under the authority of Babylon is mentioned five times to be seventy years before the Lord returns (Zechariah 1; Daniel 9; Jeremiah 25, 29; Isaiah 21–23). A sign?

The Jewish calendar contains seventy appointed times (Leviticus 23, Exodus 12).

NOTES

Section Eighteen

Other Numbers

Remember that Jesus spoke in parables and that the prophets spoke with strange visions; there are always meanings hidden in the messages. This same God uses numbers in the same way. There are messages or hidden insights into the ways of God that He wants us to see, otherwise why would it be so apparent and the same numbers be recorded throughout the history of the Scriptures, especially regarding prophecy? God is trying to tell us something through the numbers. I know this sounds bizarre, but does it really surprise you to see God's divine order documented? Isn't the sun an exact distance from the earth for human existence? Numbers puts His creation in order.

An odd number, seventeen, comes up in Jeremiah 32. Jeremiah bought property in Jerusalem for seventeen shekels while being captive in Babylon. The Lord explained that this transaction acknowledged that the Jews would return to Israel. This is while Israel is still under the authority and under the influence of Babylon that ended up being seventy years. Jeremiah had everything written, sealed, and witnessed by men.

Consider this in explaining seventeen: three times five plus two indicates a "perfect sign confirmed or bore witness to." This chapter is very important prophetically because it represented the return of the Jews during the seventy years of bondage under Babylon. In the last verse, the Lord stated He would repeat their captivity again, referring to the end times. History will repeat itself. We are in the time of the fulfillment of this prophecy being repeated.

Is the number breakdown a possibility? Using the definitions of the numbers given earlier, let's break this down a little differently. How about seven plus ten equals seventeen, or "complete holiness." How about five plus twelve as "a sign of authority" given by God to Jeremiah that the people would return to Israel? For the past few years, there has been a great influx of Jews returning to Jerusalem, and this has been especially true of Russian Jews returning to their home land of Israel. Unfortunately, they will be scattered again only to be brought back the third (perfect) time just before the coming of the Messiah. These consist of the 144,000 Jews who have been marked for God and have made it through the tribulation. It appears that there are only 7,000 men out of this group of 144,000. This could be broken down as a product of men made "righteous by complete perfection" or those who are made or accepted as "being perfectly complete by God."

We could continue to break down seventeen with different combinations, but I think the point is obvious that the numbers in numbers and God's use of mathematics seem to work when the numbers are used in context. This indicates to me the authority, the power, and the wisdom of God. He wants mankind to recognize that His hand is in everything, every detail of life, and that nothing is by mere chance. If all Scripture has a reason and is meant for correction, to explain doctrine, and to grant knowledge of God, there must be a reason specific numbers recur throughout Scriptures. We must also understand that God is consistent; He is the same today as He was yesterday. He is a God of grace, but He is also a God of judgment. That is the rest of the truth that is over looked today. We are being taught only partial truths, don't be fooled!

Another odd number mentioned is in the first book of Matthew, the recording of the genealogy of Joseph. It points out three (perfect) sets of fourteen generations to Joseph as being the father of Christ. We know he was not the biological father but the one given the authority to raise Jesus in a father's position. It is seemingly odd to me that a whole chapter is designated to Joseph when he is not the real father. The question arises why God wanted that recorded. So using numbers, here are some ideas to consider that make sense. The numbers make it clear that the numbers are in reference to Jesus, not Joseph.

Fourteen can be broken down in several ways; Seven plus seven would indicate "confirmed completion," or a "confirmed and complete cleansing;" ten plus four equals "holy judgment" or reversing the order as four plus ten to be "judgment by holiness;" twelve plus two would mean, "Authority confirmed." Let's look at two times five, plus four, equals four times one, plus ten; "a confirmed sign of judgment that equals judgment by a God of holiness." How about two times six, plus one, plus one to mean, "a confirmation to man, confirmed by God." These entire breakdowns of course are in reference to Jesus and each formula can be used on either side of the equation used. It is fascinating how the numbers are interchangeable.

All these references are about Him to be born upon completing the third set (perfect) of fourteen generations. Here is one that I like on fourteen: three plus seven, plus four, equals four times one, plus ten, interpreted as Jesus is the "perfect and complete judge that will judge by His holiness."

In Ezekiel 12 and Numbers 9, fourteen appears again. It seems for some strange reason that the fourteenth day was designated as the day to celebrate the Passover, originally a day judgment passed over them. If we compared the same breakdown of numbers regarding Passover, it somehow works again and is consistent. We can compare symbolically that Jesus is our Passover. If we submit to His authority and believe in Him, through His blood, death will pass over us. Jesus declared that He came into the world to be made perfect, in order that He could judge the world with perfection.

This writing is definitely a case of where numbers and current events come together in support of the last days. I know that it has been claimed for thousands of years the return of Jesus. I have to admit, I am not one hundred percent sure where we are in the tribulation period, but I am sure the coming of the Messiah will be within ten years. I am convinced that the reason these numbers must be understood is to help us prepare to meet our Redeemer. We must decide where we will spend eternity. There are many paths to follow in life. The purpose of this writing is not to increase our knowledge on numbers but to help us follow the numbers that lead us to Jesus. A subtitle sums it up as *Finding Jesus by Numbers.*

Other Interesting Numbers

15: Using three times five, "a perfect sign." In Genesis 7, the rain stopped when it was fifteen cubits above the highest mountaintops. Another formula format could be, five plus three, plus seven equals "a sign of perfection and completion." A question I have often wondered about is how did Noah know about the location of the mountaintops if he was to see nothing but water?

21: Daniel fasted for twenty-one days or three weeks of seven days a week, when finally Gabriel was able to deliver a message. This could be understood as he was given a "perfect and complete message" or Daniel was "perfect and complete to receive the message from the Lord." If you took two times ten, plus one, it could mean "confirmed holiness with God" that equals three times seven or "perfect completion."

33: Using three times ten, plus three, is "perfect holiness with perfection". This was Christ's age when He was crucified.

42: Using ten times four plus two, "holy judgment confirmed." This is in reference to the months of the antichrist and also is recognized as three and a half years.

45: Using four times ten, plus five "The judgment of God as a sign" in Daniel.

100: Any number times 100 broken down as ten times ten, can be interpreted as "confirmed holiness or holiness made witness to, or holiness stacked on holiness."

1,000: Any number times ten three times, "His perfect power and or holiness."

144,000: Note that in context, this is referred to as 12,000 out of each of the twelve tribes of Israel that result in a product of 144,000. One way this could be broken down is three times four, times one, times ten, times ten, times ten, times twelve, interpreted as a "perfect judgment with God's perfect holiness and confirmed authority." This is of course in reference to the number of Jews who make it through the tribulation in Revelation 7.

One third: Sometimes we see fractions to be recognized as numbers over numbers. In Revelation 8 and 9, we see the first trumpet blown bringing hail, fire, and blood (three elements). This results in, 1/3 of the earth burned up, 1/3 of the trees and all green grass is burned up. On the second trumpet's blowing, 1/3 of the sea becomes blood, 1/3 of the ships are destroyed and 1/3 of the sea life is destroyed. Upon the third trumpet being blown 1/3 of all fresh water becomes poisoned. At the blowing of the fourth (judgment) trumpet, 1/3 of the sun, 1/3 of the moon and 1/3 of the stars are stricken, and 1/3 of the daylight is kept from shining and 1/3 of the night is kept from shining. There is 1/3 of mankind killed at the blowing of the sixth (man) trumpet (Revelation 9). Isn't this an interesting use of numbers? If you were to add all the thirds up, you end up with 12/3 which equals four, which could be interpreted as, "authority over or with perfection, results in judgment," using the common denominator. If we reversed the formula to four, equals 12/3, or "judgment with authority and perfection." This is another case of the sum equaling the whole.

One fourth: Another fraction used is 1/4 of mankind destroyed: Or "God is over or in charge of judgment" (Revelation 6).

Three and a half: It did not rain for three and a half years after Elijah prayed for drought (James 5).

The two witnesses of God witness for three and one half years, killed, then after three and one half days are resurrected (Revelations 11).

The antichrist will profane the temple and claim to be God for three and a half years (Revelation). This is also referred to as forty-two months, which, broken down, signifies four times ten plus two, "a time of testing confirmed, or judgment by holiness confirmed (four times ten plus two)."

Three and a half plus three and a half equals seven, again an example of numbers in numbers. Three and a half plus three and a half signifies the "perfection of God being confirmed, resulting in completion by purification." You could also interpret the number three and a half "as a perfect God confirmed." Put this in perspective regarding the coming wrath of God. In regards to the witness', "a perfect God over two witnesses." This could also relate to the trinity the "Perfect Father God over His two witnesses' the Son and the Holy Spirit, or God bears witness to Himself."

Dates and Times of Visions Given to the Prophets

I am convinced that if one were to study the prophecies, there would be some kind of correlation between the dates of receiving the message and the prophetic events foretold. For instance, in Jeremiah 25, you have the fourth year and the first year, "judgment of God." Jeremiah recorded here that God was going to destroy Israel due to their disobedience.

In Jeremiah 45, in the fourth year, it was given to Jeremiah to proclaim that the Lord would bring evil on all flesh. Remember, four represents "judgment."

Here is a far-out one in Zechariah 1. Notice you have the date numbers of two, eleven, and twenty-four. It is recorded that an angel asked the Lord a question as to how much longer until He redeemed Israel, referring to the seventy years of indignation they will be going through. This is asked toward the end of that period of seventy years. The Lord responded by saying, "Until it is time for His return and to build the new temple." Now the recorded numbers within the reference. Two, "an event that will confirm," (ten plus one) "the holiness of God" with (two times twelve) "confirmed authority." Put together it is interpreted as "an event confirming the holiness of God with confirmed authority." This is at the end of the seven years of tribulation when the Lord returns. The numbers work!

Look at Daniel 12 verse 4, Daniel was instructed to seal up the book regarding all this information pertaining to the last days. In verse 6, Daniel asked how long it would be until all this happened. In the rest of the chapter, He was told for three and a half years (times), once the holy people were scattered. Note in the context the three and a half years are designated as a formula as follows, "one year, plus two years, plus one half a year," three distinct times of events. This could be understood as" God will confirm himself by two witnesses."

Then, upon the discontinuing of the burnt offering and the abomination of desolation, spoken of in Daniel, it will be 1,290 days, but blessed is the one who waits until the 1,335th day. Let's break this down, using the definitions of the numbers and applying them within the context. Taking 1,290 first as "God's confirmation and preparation for holiness." Then the next number 1,335 would be understood as; "God's perfect confirmation of His chosen, by signs." Also note the forty-five day difference between the two. Putting the number forty five into a formula it would be five plus four times ten. This could be interpreted as a "sign to man of judgment by holiness." The prophets were continually claiming God's judgment on people in hopes people would recognize that He is God that they might follow him.

In reference to the burnt offering, the original Hebrew wording refers to the prayers of the Jewish people at the Wailing Wall as the burnt offering. Also, note that 1,290 days in our calendar is 3.53 years and that 1,335 days is 3.66 years. This is a great exclamation point to the significance of God's use of numbers. His recorded numbers are not just by chance; this is just another way of confirming three and a half years using the Chaldean calendar.

A number of prophecies were received on specific days, dates, or times, while others were not. Why is this? I think it is obvious that the use of numbers in the Bible is for a consistent reason. It is not mystical, but it does portray the mysteries of God. This writing, I hope, has recorded some of these mysteries. Some conclusions may perhaps be stretched, or are they? Is there more to be understood? I think this is just the beginning to understanding the significance within God's numbers. What do you think? Listed below are some of the dates and numbers the prophets mention. Note the dates the visions from the Lord were given. There must be a reason those dates are significantly recorded.

Prophecies and dates to note

In the seventh year, 3,320 Jews were taken captive by Nebuchadnezzar, and in the eighteenth year, 832 Jews were taken, and in the twenty-third year, 745 Jews taken for a total of 4,600 (Jeremiah 52). This is mentioned in hopes that it will be understood in the future. I am not sure why this was recorded, but it was.

Fourteenth year of King Hezekiah of Judah (Isaiah 36).

Thirteenth year of Josiah, king of Judah, to the eleventh year of Zedekiah in the fifth month, when Jerusalem was captured (Jeremiah 1).

Fourth year of Jehoiakim, or the first year of the king of Babylon: because of Israel's disobedience, the Lord sends His servant, the king of Babylon, against Israel and the nations around Israel to destroy them. Israel is under the wings of Babylon for seventy years. After the seventy years, He will destroy Babylon (Jeremiah 25). Note the symbolism in the fourth year, a number to indicate judgment; the judgment of Israel will again be upon Israel. This passage is speaking of what is to come in the last days, as well as being pertinent in the time of Jeremiah. Note how the king is referred to as the servant of the Lord. This indicates the person chosen to make war against Israel to complete the will of God.

In the beginning of the reign of Jehoiakim, the son of Josiah, the Lord pleas for Israel to repent (Jeremiah 26).

In the beginning of the reign of Zedkiah the son of Josiah, king of Judah, Nebuchadnezzar takes over Israel. All nations will be influenced by Babylon's culture until the given day. The false prophets who speak peace will die. The people are to serve Babylon until the day the Lord returns the Jews to their homeland (Jeremiah 27).

At the beginning of Zedekiah, king of Judah in the fifth month, fourth year. The false prophet claimed peace and Jeremiah spoke against him. Hananiah, the false prophet, dies in the seventh month of that year (Jeremiah 28).

In the tenth year of Zedekiah, king of Judah, and the eighteenth year of Nebuchadnezzar: Jeremiah bought property in Israel for seventeen shekels (Jeremiah 32).

In the fourth year, Jehoakim, the son of Josiah, king of Judah, a scroll was eaten by Jeremiah that contained the words of God that were not to be revealed (Jeremiah 36).

In the ninth year of Zedekiah, the king of Judah, in the tenth month: Nebuchadnezzar comes against Jerusalem (Jeremiah 39).

The fourth year of Jehoiakim, the son of Josiah, king of Judah: The Lord proclaimed to bring evil on all flesh (Jeremiah 45; note again the fourth year, or judgment).

Thirtieth year, fourth month, fifth day: Ezekiel sees a vision of four angels; each had four faces and four wings. He also sees four wheels within the wheels being rolled by the angels (Ezekiel 1).These numbers are symbolic in reference to the timing of the end, the judgment of God. Number thirty as "Perfect holiness," fourth month, "by judgment", fifth day, "to be a sign to man."

In the sixth year, sixth month, fifth day: the abominations of Israel are revealed (Ezekiel 8).

Seventh year, fifth month, tenth day: the abominations of Israel are revealed to the elders (Ezekiel 20).

Ninth year, tenth month, and tenth day: the day Babylon comes against Jerusalem and the allegory of the boiling pot (Ezekiel 24).

Eleventh year, first day of the month: the sea will destroy Tyre (Ezekiel 26).

Tenth year, tenth month, twelfth day: a prophecy against Egypt, they shall be a desolation and a wasteland (Ezekiel 29).

Twentieth and seventh years, first month, first day, and eleventh year, first month, and seventh day: Egypt is given over to Babylon (Ezekiel 29).

Eleventh year, third month, first day: the fall of Egypt. Egypt is compared to a large cedar tree that is destroyed by the most terrible of the nations by war (Ezekiel 31).

Twelfth year, twelfth month, on the first day: evils come upon the king of Egypt (Ezekiel 32). The last Babylon comes against Egypt and Egypt is destroyed.

Twelfth year, first month, fifteenth day, Egypt joins the other nations of the world in the pit (Ezekiel 32).

Twelfth year, tenth month, fifth day of exile: Israel will be destroyed by war and made desolate. The people worship the Lord with their lips, but their hearts are set on selfish gain (Ezekiel 33).

Twenty-fifth year of exile, first month, tenth day, fourteenth year after Jerusalem was conquered: the new temple is described (Ezekiel 40).

First month on the fourteenth day: Jews are to go for seven days eating unleavened bread to celebrate Passover. In the seventh month, fifteenth day: seven days of feast are to be celebrated (Ezekiel 45).

Third year of Jehoakim, king of Judah: Babylon seized Jerusalem (Daniel 1).

Second year of Nebuchadnezzar: he had a dream of a man with clay and iron feet. This represents the fourth ruling empire of Babylon designated to be in the last days (Daniel 2).

First year of Belshazzar, king of Babylon: Daniel saw a vision of four beasts that came out of the sea and saw the throne of God. It is revealed to him that there is one, the fourth beast that comes against the Lord and makes war on the saints (Daniel 7).

Third year of King Belshazzar: Daniel received a vision of a goat and a ram and the interpretation is given by Gabriel (Daniel 8).

First year of Darius, a Mede, and king of the Chaldeans: Daniel was given confirmation about the seventy years that Jerusalem will be under Babylon's authority only to be betrayed and destroyed (Daniel 9).

Third year of Cyrus, king of Persia: Daniel was given an understanding of what was to come in the last days (Daniel 10).

First year of Darius, the Mede: Four kings will come out of Persia, the fourth being the strongest; here, the antichrist is described (Daniel 11).

Second year, sixth month, first day of Darius: the call to rebuild the temple (Haggai 1).

Second year, seventh month, twenty-first day of Darius: the Lord shall shake the heavens and the earth again (Haggai 2).

Second year, ninth month, twenty-fourth day of Darius: There will be a time in which the Lord will bless Israel (Haggai 2).

Second year, eighth month of Darius: Israel is called to repent (Zechariah 1).

Second year, eleventh month, twenty-fourth day of Darius: the question is asked of the Lord as to how much longer Jerusalem and Judah will have to bear these three score and ten (seventy) years of God's anger. The Lord states He will return and build His new temple (Zechariah 6). Zechariah is shown four skilled destroyers that scatter Israel (Zechariah 1). This could possibly be the four mentioned in Daniel 11.

Fourth year, ninth month, fourth day of king Darius: the Lord rebukes those who have fasted for seventy years in the fifth and seventh months because they are fasting for themselves, they are not seeking God, but they fast to impress others. (Zechariah 7).

NOTES

Section Nineteen

Numbers in Judaism

The importance of numbers are significantly recognized in Judaism. Jews firmly believe each number has a definition; some are a result of the sum of numbers, and others are the product of numbers. It is interesting to note the similarity of Judaism and the text within *Jesus by Numbers*. It is also important to notice the differences.

Many of the definitions this writing is based on come from the New Testament. The Jews are limited in their understanding of numbers without the New Testament, which help to clarify the meanings of numbers in the Old Testament. Here are only a few numbers and their Jewish meanings. They have over two hundred definitions of numbers. When it comes to numbers, they understand the power of numbers comprised of numbers within numbers. They claim, "The sum equals the whole."

Three symbolizes "holiness or fulfillment."

Four is the result of adding three plus one, which symbolizes "divine revelation," "fulfillment of God's plan."

Six represents "imperfection."

Seven represents "the covenant of holiness and sanctification, holy, the divine number of completion."

Eight represents a "new beginning."

Ten represents "absolute completeness."

Twelve, the product of three times four, represents the "union of people with God."

Eighteen is the product of certain numbers that represent "life." Compare this to the product of 666, or three times six to symbolize the seeking for; "fulfillment of man's life."

Thirty, three times ten represents "perfection of divine order". For the Jews when one reaches the age of thirty, they reach the prime of their energy.

Forty represents "trials and testing" and has two breakdowns for definitions, four times ten and five times eight. It represents a transition or change, the concept of renewal, or a new beginning. It has the power to lift the spiritual state, to begin spiritual renewal. It also represents the four sides of the world, each containing ten powers.

Seventy represents the seventy evil forces that are against Israel. It also represents the "sum of the parts, the whole, ultimate completeness." It is the product of seven magnified by ten.

There are seventy qualities to be sought in the Torah. Those who find all seventy are complete in God. For them, seventy also represents conflict between the seventy world nations and the Jewish people that will determine the destiny of the world. The Jewish people claim they are chosen for leading mankind toward universal acceptance of God as the one and only God. The final end of creation is when Israel, while observing the Torah, returns to Jerusalem, the city of holiness, in the worship of God.

Jews believe there are seventy names for Israel. Seventy names of the Torah and seventy names for Jerusalem. When all these names or parts come together, it will result in a unified state of wholeness. Note the three sets of seventy names to achieve "fulfillment, holiness and divine completion." Mathematically I would recognize that when the three sets of seventy names come together in the end as, "a perfect timing of events to complete His holiness."

They believe Israel will be the catalyst that unites the seventy dispersed nations to fulfill the seventy facets of the Torah. This will result in the revealing of the oneness of God in the messianic era: "On that day, God will be one and His name shall be one."

They also believe there are seventy angels ruling over Israel. It is also interesting to note that they have a total of seventy days a year that are holy days designated for celebration.

Something Weird

This is weird, and I do not know how to explain this. This discovery of God's number system took me about seven years. During that time, something very strange occurred during a period of four to five weeks. At first, I thought it mere coincidence; I will let you decide. I experienced four times, in which the computer monitor went black with large words in blue appearing on the screen. I thought it to be just an accident the first two times, which were about seven to ten days apart. The first time I read **"time is short**." The second time that words appeared said **"seventy years."** The third time, I read, "**The wrath of God on all flesh."** The fourth message simply stated "**Number 4"** which remember means **judgment**. When these words and phrases appeared, they lasted about a minute before disappearing. I remember one time that I had not even opened anything; I just turned on the computer. It was strange!

One can conclude that time is indeed short. This may be an unpopular and uncomfortable conclusion, but the day of the Lord is nearer than we think. It is time for the holiness of God and the destiny of man to collide. Man has exchanged the holiness of God for his own comforts. It is currently a time the Jews believe that seventy nations of the world shall come against them. This is necessary to usher in the Messiah and Israel being saved for the last time. I could be wrong on the timing; however, the events will happen. Besides, what if I am right?

I have written this book in hopes that it will open your mind and stimulate your thoughts every time you read and study God's Word. It is also meant to increase your knowledge of God, resulting in an increase in the depth of your walk with Him. It is not written to tickle the ears, meaning not to be politically correct with the word of God, but to reveal the truth of God. I hope that lies are exposed and we allow God to direct our paths to help us navigate through life. My hopes are that we are not deceived, destroyed or distracted but that our hearts would be directed toward God. That we would understand our purpose in life and discover God for who He really is by challenging our hearts. My hope is that our hearts would be strengthened that we may endure and persevere when testing comes. For I fear that many Christians have exchanged truth for lies, that we have replaced God with ourselves. I pray that we may increase in the wisdom of God, and that our desire to seek him would dominate our lives. That we would learn to resist temptation. This study on numbers I hope reveals a deeper meaning of the numbers used in the Bible and the parables of Christ. That we would fear God and have a strong foundation in the knowledge of God.

Through numbers, we discovered the trinity. How the crucifixion perfectly demonstrated discipline. That we are to pick up the cross daily and die to our personal selfish desires. We should have a better understanding of the last days, the meaning behind the number 666. Through numbers the grace, and the judgment of God is revealed. Understanding we have religiously become polluted by denying the power of Christ. We have tainted God's grace. The moral laws of God have been replaced with the immoral laws of man, and we accept them.

The Bible is about characters and people, their lives, how they relate to us today. Numbers are the characters in *Jesus by Numbers*, revealing the character of God, yesterday and today. By understanding the importance and meaning of numbers within His Living Word, will define the person of Jesus, salvation and grace. Understanding numbers will redefine our walk with him. The goal of this writing is that we all do a self-evaluation of our walk with Christ, rediscover the joy of His salvation with excitement, and discover the ways, the mysteries, and the awesomeness of God. In doing so, we will overcome the ways of the world only to hear "well done my good and faithful servant."

Also, understand the authenticity of the numbers in God's word is not new; it has just been overlooked for some reason. Then there is the number seventy spoke of so often by the prophets, the end of sin and the return of Jesus. I hope that it makes sense now. It all begins with God, number one. It ends with the number seventy or seven times ten, times one, with "complete holiness of God." That is the message in the numbers, putting an end to sin.

God bless you, and have fun studying numbers in His Word.

Time is short! Remember to keep the faith, persevere, and be in continuous prayer, watching for His return.